THE
Customer
Service
ACTIVITY
BOOK

THE
Customer
Service
ACTIVITY
BOOK

50 ACTIVITIES FOR INSPIRING
EXCEPTIONAL SERVICE

Darryl S. Doane
Rose D. Sloat

AMACOM

AMERICAN MANAGEMENT ASSOCIATION
New York | Atlanta | Brussels | Chicago | Mexico City | San Francisco
Shanghai | Tokyo | Toronto | Washington, D. C.

This publication is designed to provide accurate and authoritative information in regard to the subject matter covered. It is sold with the understanding that the publisher is not engaged in rendering legal, accounting, or other professional service. If legal advice or other expert assistance is required, the services of a competent professional person should be sought.

Library of Congress Cataloging-in-Publication Data

Doane, Darryl S.
    The customer service activity book : 50 activities for inspiring exceptional
service / Darryl S. Doane, Rose D. Sloat.
        p.   cm.
    Rev. ed. of: 50 activities for achieving excellent customer service / Rose D. Sloat, c2002.
    Includes bibliographical references and index.
    ISBN 0-8144-7259-1 (alk. paper)
    1. Customer services.   2. Service industries workers—Training of.   I. Title: 50 activities
for inspiring exceptional service.   II. Title: Inspiring exceptional service.   III. Sloat, Rose D.
IV. Doane, Darryl S. 50 activities for achieving excellent customer service.   V. Title.

HF5415.5.D58   2005
658.8'12—dc22
                                                                        2004030704

Printing number

10 9 8 7 6 5 4 3 2

DEDICATION

To my wife, Anne, our children Diana Doane
and Adam and his wife, Lisa Doane

Darryl S. Doane

To my husband, Al, our children Julie Sloat
and Valerie and her husband, Jamie Garrett,
and grandson, Drew

Rose D. Sloat

CONTENTS

HANDOUTS, OVERHEADS, AND WORKSHEETS

PDF files of these materials are also available online at http://www.amacombooks.org/CustServActivity

INTRODUCTION

A New Revolution in Customer Service

Did you ever hear of someone throwing a party and no one coming? The revolutionary ideas that have struck such a note of excitement and encouragement in the customer service arena for 15 years—*the customer is number one; every decision made within a company should be made with the customer in mind, the customer needs to be the central figure of any organization*—have left many feeling just that way. So much was planned and strategized, making expectations high. Unfortunately, these expectations were not met, and now the customer has raised the ante. Many expectations have now become demands.

This manual will help your participants respond to the following customer demands:

- Make my life easier

- Focus on me

- Help me to be more successful

- Respond to my needs

- Build a responsive relationship with me

- Know my problems and provide solutions

Part A, "Service Attitude," and Part D, "Professionalism with No Excuses," provide activities that will enable you to take this new customer service revolution to your participants.

The activities will emphasize your customers' new demands, as well as the individual and team attitude necessary to support and deliver the required service.

What This Resource Manual Provides

1. Activities that are sensitive to the new revolution taking place in customer service and in meeting customer demands.

2. Identification and creation of memorable experiences for your customer service representatives and their customers.

3. A valuable treasure of resources whether you are a seasoned veteran, a trainer/ facilitator with middle-of-the-road years of experience, or a newcomer or occasional trainer.

4. Fifty effective activities that may be easily aligned with the specific needs and identified competencies within your customer service area.

5. User-friendly activities that take you step-by-step through the training process, allowing you to deliver high-impact training that easily makes a difference.

6. Activities that are customized to your needs and include a number of variations and additional insights and ideas to make them the "right fit" for your programs.

7. A Documenter to identify and develop your own customized collection of customer service interactions within your organization.

8. Powerful bonus sections to complement and support your customer service core values and enhance performance.

9. Effective tools to assist you in attaining the next level of success with the individual who needs to be your primary focus—the Customer!

A Memorable Experience

The relationships you build with your customers must become memorable experiences in the customer's mind to create customer hunger for your style of service and caring that results in repeat business. As such, your training experience also needs to be memorable, leaving your customer service participants with the necessary knowledge, skills, and ability to complement and enhance performance by professionally transferring what was learned in the classroom setting to everyday behavior in the workplace.

The activities in Part G, "Essential Tools for Success," are specifically designed to support and enhance that memorable experience through the evaluation of the workplace environment and the best customer service practices. Part J, "Fulfilling Needs/Providing Solutions," focuses on building customer confidence, encouraging participants to get to know customers so well that they can anticipate and appropriately respond to their changes, needs, and problems. Parts G and J focus on and specifically target the business and industrial arenas and their customers. The activities are intended to raise to a higher level of conscious awareness the creativity, interaction, participation, knowledge, and skill level of those you have chosen to have primary contact with the customer, your organization's most precious commodity. These learning experiences have been selected to validate, complement, support, and reinforce your existing and developing training programs, concentrating on that individual who must be the critical epicenter of your organization— the customer.

The Seasoned Trainer

For the seasoned trainer, this manual offers a variety of approaches for delivering your message to your people. Taken together, the activities provide a treasure of resources that could easily be used as a complete customer service training program or could be adapted to include in your own programs. Each activity is deigned to create enthusiasm, intensify focus, and raise the level of awareness of a critical area of customer service. The knowledge and skills identified with each activity may be easily aligned with your recognized competencies and placed into appropriate programs or learning experiences. These activities are wonderful for training staff, organizational learning department, corporate university, or individual facilitators who are looking to add to their existing customer service base. The manual is flexible to your needs and programs. New, fresh approaches can revitalize and reenergize not only participants, but the training staff itself.

This manual addresses the issue of *blended learning.* It easily moves from traditional, stand-up, highly interactive activities such as "The People in Your Office" (Part F) to high-quality assessments and instrumented learning tools such as the Understanding Our DISC Style (Part K) and "Putting Your Company to the Test: Being Your Own Customer" (Part H). Thus, for a seasoned, veteran trainer, this manual contains a plethora of easily acceptable, useful tools.

The New or Occasional Trainer

Those of you who are new to your organization's training department will find this resource manual invaluable. As you develop your customer service programs, what a benefit to have such a valuable collection of activities, which have been proven to get results. And, if you are only an occasional trainer with time constraints and demands on your schedule, what a powerful tool this becomes to enhance your own productivity and allow you to deliver high-quality activities.

Whether a new or occasional trainer, you probably have an ideal picture of what customer service should deliver. We've all heard the expressions: a blinding flash of the obvious, good old common sense, and the golden rule, "Do unto others as you would have them do unto you." These reflect the feelings we've all had about what customer service should be. Unfortunately, we have also walked away shaking our heads disgusted, bewildered, dazed, and confused after receiving less than adequate customer service. It should be so simple. Treat the customer as you would a guest in your own home. The customer is number one. There would be no business without the customer. The customer needs to be the center of your organization.

We should know better, but still poor service continues—inadequate care for what the customer wants, which is solutions, results, and the fulfillment of their needs. And, yes, the problem has even carried over to the information age. The World Wide Web confuses, abuses, and loses customer after customer, and the results are devastating. Customers take their business elsewhere as they maneuver through the electronic debris of companies that quickly rose only to suddenly fall as they ignored the obvious: focus on the customer!

This resource manual is dedicated to awakening and strengthening that level of customer focus that simply must exist if any business wishes to continue to survive and ultimately prosper. Here, you will find the very best activities to support and complement your customer service development. We have gathered them from our respected peers in the training arena, as well as from our own collection of activities.

The Customer Service Documenter

The Documenter allows you to customize your organization's own customer service experiences for future reference through training, role plays, new-hire orientation, group discussions, and a myriad of learning experiences. The template sets the stage for easily creating your own library and resource of customer service situations from within your own company. Please refer to Appendix A to begin your own customized collection of documented customer service interactions for your organization.

Biographies

At the back of the manual, you will find biographies of the individuals who contributed activities to this manual. It has been difficult to attribute all activities to a particular source. Every effort has been made to do this wherever possible. Colleagues were asked to submit their most successful, beneficial, and "best" customer service activity to us for consideration. Those selected have been credited and acknowledged. We thank everyone who contributed and whose submission(s) were selected for use, as well as those whose submissions were not included. We believe that the final result is truly a reflection of the collected wisdom, gifts, and talents of all those who took part in this endeavor. We thank all of you for your time and dedication to the continued quest to achieve excellent customer service.

HOW TO USE THIS RESOURCE MANUAL

This manual is divided into thirteen activity areas. Each has been subdivided into the following components so that the activity may be easily aligned with the specific needs and identified competencies a trainer/facilitator/in-house training staff may have. We recommend that you familiarize yourself with the entire manual and its areas of concentration. Simply align the area with your particular customer service focus by selecting the activity that best reflects the direction you have established for your participants to move in.

Trainers may use the handouts, overheads, and worksheets to complement and support their presentations of the materials in the following manner.

Handouts are reference sheets that can be used as a resource or a tool for individual or group activities. They also reinforce the skills covered in the activity.

The **overheads** are tools used to relay key points of the activity. They can also be used as a guide for the facilitator and the participants as they move through the activity.

The information in them may be presented as an overhead transparency, may be written on a flip chart or dry erase board, or may be transposed to PowerPoint.

Worksheets assist in the implementation of an activity and are used to gather responses and answers to questions, for taking notes, for stimulating discussions, and for practicing the skills of the activity. They are also intended to customize the activity and its benefits for a particular group.

These materials along with the Documenter and Customer Service Reminders, will also be available to you on the Web (see page x). This is provided with the intention of reinforcing and complementing the knowledge and skills of the activity with which they are associated.

ACTIVITY DESCRIPTION (WITH TIME GUIDELINE)

What is this activity all about? What does it concentrate or focus on? What does it promote (i.e., discussion, actions, particular behavior, awakening, etc.)? How much time is required for this particular activity?

LEARNING OBJECTIVES

- Purpose

- Participants will be able to . . .

- Benefits

METHOD OF INSTRUCTION

- Materials needed

- Preparation and room set-up

- Step-by-step walk-through of the activity

NOTES, INSIGHTS, AND VARIATIONS (OPTIONAL)

- How to make the activity as effective as possible

- Tips for fine tuning from the originators or those who have actually performed the activity

- Other applications, approaches, and/or items to include or be aware of to ensure success

Service Attitude

Your attitude permeates absolutely everything you do. You own your attitude, and it establishes and reflects your professionalism, caring, focus, and passion to deliver excellent customer service. This is demonstrated every day with each customer contact.

This activity area of concentration was intentionally placed first because if you do not have the proper attitude to propel you forward, the other components to achieve excellent customer service simply will not happen. You may possess an incredible knowledge of your company and services provided. You may have the skills to make that knowledge come alive. But, without the attitude or caring to take action, the proper service will still not happen.

Attitude Check 1

Activity Description

TIME GUIDELINE: 20 MINUTES

This activity concentrates on reinforcing, coaching, and supporting the skills and knowledge learned in a program. It promotes camaraderie, positive behavior, and an awareness that "we are in this together" and "you aren't alone."

Learning Objectives

PURPOSE:

This activity promotes a positive, enthusiastic follow up and mutual reinforcement to the training that takes place.

PARTICIPANTS WILL BE ABLE TO:

1. Demonstrate that training is an ongoing, continuous process of learning that does not end abruptly when a training session is formally over.

2. Identify the critical role each person plays in the learning process through coaching, reinforcing, and mastering, to support and encourage each other.

3. Recognize the critical role *attitude* plays in making one's knowledge and skills effective.

BENEFITS:

Individuals can rely on one of their peers as a coach, mentor, or someone to share concerns with, and to reinforce the knowledge and skills of the program presented.

Method of Instruction

MATERIALS NEEDED

Paper (various colors)
Pens

PREPARATION AND ROOM SET-UP

No additional preparation is required. The activity is applicable to whatever room set-up the presenter has selected.

STEP-BY-STEP WALK-THROUGH OF THE ACTIVITY

Step 1: Hand out a piece of paper (various colors) to each participant.

Step 2: On the paper, each participant should write the following, so that they can be contacted after the program is completed:

Name

Contact information

Phone number

Address

E-mail

Step 3: After participants provide the appropriate information—and please stress the importance of this—have them crumple up their paper into a ball.

Step 4: Ask them to stand and form a circle.

Step 5: When they hear our signal (use a bell, whistle, verbal instruction, etc.), they should throw the crumpled paper into the inner circle.

Step 6: Retrieve one of the pieces of tossed paper and throw it.

Step 7: Continue with this until papers are thoroughly mixed up (about 1.5 minutes).

Step 8: Have them stop, pick up a paper, and open it without sharing the contents. That individual whose name is written on the paper has now become their person to coach, mentor, check up on, reinforce skills with, and communicate with.

Step 9: Select a contact date two to three weeks away. Remind them that we are all teachers and students and to please accept the responsibility to contact that individual whose name has come into their possession on that date.

Step 10: Divide the group into teams of four to six, select a team leader, and have each group create a list of questions to ask and things to share when the contact is made. Ask them how they can help each other to take the knowledge and skills learned in the class and transfer them to the "real world," making them part of their normal everyday behavior (allow five to eight minutes).

Step 11: Have each group present their results, writing the responses on a "master list."

Notes, Insights, and Variations

- You may wish to have participants identify whose name each person has. This tends to create more accountability.

- When in teams, you may have each group also create a second list entitled, "As your coach/mentor, what should you expect from me?"

Whose Attitude 2

Activity Description

TIME GUIDELINE: 25 MINUTES

This activity is designed as a case study for the trainer to read aloud and then use to lead a discussion as to how each participant or his/her organization would handle it. The story is true, and in most cases, "we've all been there."

Learning Objectives

PURPOSE:

This activity promotes the power of a positive attitude in a customer service situation.

PARTICIPANTS WILL BE ABLE TO:

1. Promote interaction among group members to discuss how the customer should have been treated.

2. Identify poor customer service and how it should have been avoided.

BENEFITS:

Participants will have the realization that attitude permeates all that a person does and that it carries over to the customer's perception of the service he/she receives.

Method of Instruction

MATERIALS NEEDED

The story by LP of Green Bay, Wisconsin
Flip chart
Markers to record participant's comments

PREPARATION AND ROOM SET-UP

No additional preparation is required. This activity is applicable to whatever room set-up the presenter has selected.

STEP-BY-STEP WALK-THROUGH OF THE ACTIVITY

Step 1: Read this story by LP of Green Bay, Wisconsin, aloud—or have one of the participants read the story.

> About a year ago, I went to a large department store in the evening. Although I realized it was 8:45 p.m. and the stored closed at 9:00 p.m., I really needed to buy four director's chairs. The chair department had only two on the floor, so I asked a member of the sales staff if they had two more of the chairs. She told me that nothing was left on the floor to match the color and style I wanted.
>
> When she failed to offer to check the stock room, I asked if they had any in stock. With a big sigh, she told me she would have to call down to the stock room and find out. When she did call, she found out they had two more of the kind I wanted. She then asked if I really wanted them. I replied that, of course, I did!
>
> "Well," she said, "it's going to take some time and we're almost closing."
> I indicated that I was willing to wait.
>
> She then told the person in the stock room to bring them up, resignedly saying, "This lady wants them!"
>
> "Thank you," I said, "and I hope this isn't going to be too much of a problem for you."
>
> I meant this sincerely, but the clerk obviously didn't like the comment. "You know, lady," she said, "you really have an attitude problem."

At this point, I said I would be right back to get my chairs and I walked over to the customer service department, a short distance from where I had been standing. When I reported the incident, the chairs were quickly brought up. But I never shopped at that store again, and I have often shared this story, so that this one bad customer service incident has been heard by many people.*

Step 2: Identify the poor customer service elements in the above story.

Step 3: Discuss how the customer should have been treated.

Step 4: Compare the participants' discussion with the response below:

The Telephone "Doctor"®'s Response

There are so many obvious bad points in this story. First of all, retailers that get customers at the last moment need to ensure that all their employees realize that this could be the "sale of the day!" Consumers rarely notice the time when they're out shopping. This is true especially when they have something special in mind, a mission. This particular shopper noticed the time—and also knew exactly what she wanted. She hadn't come in to browse.

Secondly, it seems to be a common problem to "have to check the stock room." Hey, that's retail—checking to see if you have what the customer needs. As for the "big sigh," those negative audible noises are the first step toward poor customer service. A BIG SMILE would have been the thing to do here.

To tell the customer, "It's almost closing," you might as well have told her to turn around and walk out. When a customer comes in near closing time, the first thing you need to do is let them know you'll be delighted to help them. Set the stage first, then whatever you need to tell them after that is taken far better.

This particular shopper did one thing more than I would have done. I would have walked out. She waited for the chairs. Lucky for the store.

However, judging from the last few lines of her letter, she won't be back there again. And how many others did she tell about this department store's poor service? My guess is more than we'll ever know!

*Excerpt from Customer Service Nightmares by Nancy Friedman, The Telephone "Doctor"®

Notes, Insights, and Variations

When a participant's response matches up with the Telephone "Doctor"®'s answer, a prize of some sort can be given. Nothing terribly fancy. It could be a candy bar, a free video rental, or something else the company can spare free—even a 30-minute leave early for one time. That's where a facilitator's imagination comes in handy.

Both Sides of Change 3

Activity Description

TIME GUIDELINE: 20 MINUTES

This activity promotes acceptance and understanding of change. So many people view change as a negative. This activity reminds participants that change can be positive and can represent survival and growth.

Learning Objectives

PURPOSE:

Besides constantly focusing on delivering excellent customer service, we must also deal with the challenge of change, as with new policies, a new coworker, upsizing, downsizing, mergers, acquisitions, a new boss, new responsibilities, and on and on and on. The purpose of this activity is to promote understanding, acceptance, and the realization that change is often positive and necessary.

PARTICIPANTS WILL BE ABLE TO:

1. List both positive and negative aspects of change.

2. Conclude that one can have a positive mindset when it comes to change.

BENEFITS:

A valuable benefit is the awareness that change is not always a negative, but can often be a positive reflecting growth—something comfortable and an addition rather than a loss.

Method of Instruction

MATERIALS NEEDED

Flip chart

Markers

Items such as a book, a hat, or a pair of gloves to use as props to hand to individuals during the activity

PREPARATION AND ROOM SET-UP

No additional preparation is required. This activity is applicable to whatever room set-up the presenter has selected.

STEP-BY-STEP WALK-THROUGH OF THE ACTIVITY

Step 1: Pair up the participants.

Step 2: Give them the following directions:

    A.   Stand face to face with your partner.

    B.   For 30 seconds, concentrate on your partner, noting clothing, hair style, glasses, etc.

    C.   Turn your back to each other and in the next 45 seconds change three things about your appearance.

        Hint: Remove your watch; take a shoe off, etc.

    D.   Now, turn and face each other. Identify those things your partner has changed about him or herself.

Step 3: After approximately 2 minutes, have participants take their seats.

Step 4:   Then talk about the activity you just performed.

Ask: How many of you removed something?

How many of you added something?

Note: Usually there are considerably more participants who have removed rather than added.

Step 5:   On a flip chart or overhead, put the following:

Negative	**Positive**
Taking away	Growth
Loss	Addition
Uncomfortable	Comfortable

Step 6:   Refer to the information on the chart and say:

"When a change comes along, we have a tendency to think of it with a negative mindset. Most change, even good change, is usually met with resistance at first. And, that negative mindset makes us focus on (refer to chart) a taking away, a loss, something that is gone, and it is usually thought of as an uncomfortable situation (we don't like being knocked out of our comfort zone.)"

"You are encouraged to have a more positive mindset because change is not always negative *(refer to the positive side of the chart).* Change can be positive. It can represent growth rather than a taking away. It can be an addition rather than a loss, and it can actually result in a more comfortable situation rather than the uncomfortable feeling usually associated with change.

"I'm going to ask you to fold your arms. Now take your arms apart. Now I would like you to put your arms together again, but do it in reverse. Reverse the way you usually would fold your arms. Notice how it feels very awkward *(refer to the chart again—comfortable versus uncomfortable).* We do not like to be knocked out of our comfort zone; so, we have a tendency, at least initially, to view a change as negative, wrong, or strange. We tend to dwell on the negatives.

"When you view change, we encourage you to realize that there is another option *(refer to the positive side of the chart)* and that is that a positive mindset can be a powerful force in dealing effectively with change."

Step 7: Ask the participants to give one example of how they have handled change at the workplace.

Notes, Insights, and Variations

When the participants are turned back to back in the activity and changing things about themselves, have a few items such as a book, a hat, a pair of gloves to give to individuals. This will assist in your discussion of change. Change can represent an addition, growth, and new things to be excited about.

Customer Service Icebreakers

Whether your attendees are seasoned veterans, those with middle of the road experience, or even rookies (i.e., those who are very new to the whole customer service arena and possibly even the organization they are employed with), it's very important to put people at ease and encourage their involvement and sharing of ideas. You also want to avoid divisions within your program.

This activity area does just what it states: it breaks the ice to open the door to communication, involvement, and sharing. It taps the wisdom, talents, and gifts each individual brings to the workplace. This area of concentration also allows individuals to realize that they do not stand alone but are a critical component of the entire team representing excellent customer service. These activities will get your program underway and heading in the *right* direction.

Activity Description

TIME GUIDELINE: 15 MINUTES

This activity promotes immediate involvement and immersion into the learning process. Participants will demonstrate teamwork, understanding, and cooperation before they even sit down. It reflects the importance of sharing the workload and delegating tasks to all involved in the process. Finally, it will allow for a creative mix at each location within your training session.

Learning Objectives

PURPOSE:

The main purpose of this demonstration is to bring together the participants in a cooperative, focused manner, and evenly distribute the level of expertise within each team.

PARTICIPANTS WILL BE ABLE TO:

1. Demonstrate the need to work together to accomplish a task.

2. Identify a leader and demonstrate the importance of being a cooperative follower.

3. Understand that it is easier to work together than to "go it alone" to succeed.

4. Acknowledge that the program will be educational and enjoyable.

BENEFITS:

The activity points out the value of teamwork. We need each other in order to fulfill the needs of our customers. As leaders, we need to be able to delegate to get the job done.

Method of Instruction

MATERIALS NEEDED

Classroom tables to accommodate participants (round tables preferably)

PREPARATION AND ROOM SET-UP

Select an area in the training room where participants can form a single straight line. Instruct them to line themselves up according to the years of service they have within their organization, starting with the individual with the most years of service. Designate where that individual should position himself or herself.

STEP-BY-STEP WALK-THROUGH OF THE ACTIVITY

Step 1: Instruct the rest of the group to communicate among itself.

Step 2: While still lined up, have each participant say the number of years of service aloud for all to hear. Thank them and then ask them to remember the number you assign to them.

Step 3: Count to the number of tables. For example, 5 tables means you want to count to 5 and then repeat the process in the line, assigning one number to each person. When finished, announce that those with #1 are to sit at a particular table (which you now identify), #2 at this table, #3 at another, and so on. Participants should now take their seats.

Step 4: Now, ask them what they just did. "What happened? Why did we do it?"

Suggested answers:

- It divided up the years of service at each table with a good balance to promote a good mix of ideas.
- It demonstrated good teamwork and cooperation to get the job done.

Step 5: Now, ask them to take a good look at the team members at their table. Instruct them to point at the most responsible-looking team member at the count of 3. Say, 1, 2, 3, go! Majority rules. Instruct the newly delegated team leader to delegate some responsibilities to the other members of their team. This is an excellent time to have each team get their own books, materials, whatever they need for your particular program. Each team member should be delegated a task.

Step 6: Again ask, "What happened? Why did we do it?"

Step 7: Then say,

> "In the world of customer service there is so much to accomplish. We can't go it alone. We can't do it all by ourselves. We definitely need each other to get the job done and fulfill the needs of our customers. Also, depending on our talents, knowledge, and skills, we will be called upon at times to a role of leadership. In that capacity we need to utilize the rest of the team. As followers, we need to cooperate and support the leader realizing we may assume that role at any given time and will request the support of the team at that time."

Notes, Insights, and Variations

When sharing the number of years of service, you may want to make note and add up the total to share with the group. No one can ever take away those years of work, dedication, and experience, and it represents a tremendous amount of wisdom that we want to bring out in the program. Please allow yourself to share that wisdom.

This is such a great way to get all participants interactively involved, working together, and having fun right from the get go while making some critical points. It sets the stage for ongoing involvement and cooperation throughout your workshop. Everyone realizes that their participation helps the entire group succeed. This could be a good way to begin discussing that excellent customer service should be everyone's job. Ask, "What happens when an individual does not pull their weight or do their part?"

Possible answer:

■ Raises stress, anxiety, frustrations, workload of entire group

Ask, "What happens when each individual does his or her part?"

Possible answers:

- Lowers anxiety, stress, frustrations
- Makes for a better work environment

Promoting Communications and Teamwork 5

Activity Description

TIME GUIDELINE: 20 MINUTES

When a group of people are brought together for training in a seminar or workshop, they have varying levels of familiarity with each other. This can be true if the people are all from one company or if they are a mixed group, such as a combination of suppliers and customers. In either case, this exercise is an excellent icebreaker that promotes bonding and enables people to get to know each other and to share personal information that everyone can relate to so they can better understand one another.

Learning Objectives

PURPOSE:

The objective of this activity is to promote bonding between participants and encourage the sharing of information.

PARTICIPANTS WILL BE ABLE TO:

1. Create an atmosphere of openness and familiarity.

2. Provide a learning environment.

BENEFITS:

As stated in the title, the activity promotes communications and teamwork. The learning process is accelerated through the creation of an environment that complements and supports learning.

Method of Instruction

MATERIALS NEEDED

8.5 × 11 sheets of paper
Tape or adhesive

PREPARATION AND ROOM SET-UP

Before the group arrives, mount the paper on the walls in the four corners of the room. Write one of the following on each piece of paper: Oldest child, Middle child, Youngest child, Only child.

STEP-BY-STEP WALK-THROUGH OF THE ACTIVITY

Step 1: After some introductions, tell the participants to go to the corner of the room that defines them. (Only children will always go to the "only child" corner, even though they are also the oldest.)

Step 2: Once they have gone to their proper place, ask them to spend 10 minutes or so (depending on how many people there are) taking turns discussing how their birth order affected how they were treated and how it affects where they are today and how they think about things.

   Usually the stories and perspectives they share will be very similar, and the result is usually lots of laughs and insights, while a natural bonding takes place because of these shared experiences.

Step 3: While still in their corners, but after they all have had a chance to talk, have each group tell the other groups what the members discussed.

   Usually the groups will cast dispersions at each other in a good-hearted way during this phase of the exercise, and it promotes a very relaxed start for the rest of the gathering while helping people become closer.

Who Are You? 6

Activity Description

TIME GUIDELINE: 30 MINUTES

This activity promotes group togetherness and the realization that there is strength in both similarities and differences.

Learning Objectives

PURPOSE:

This activity encourages the participants to work together, open up, and share ideas—to create an atmosphere of functioning as a team while demonstrating individual differences.

PARTICIPANTS WILL BE ABLE TO:

1. Identify words that reflect their own personality.

2. Explain to others how the word they choose reflects their own behavior.

BENEFITS:

The activity provides a springboard for additional discussion on such topics as leadership, teamwork, and behavior.

Method of Instruction

MATERIALS NEEDED

Four sets of 5" × 10" cards with the following words on them:

Set 1
A. Competitive
B. Compromising
C. Collaborative
D. Accommodating

Set 3
A. Caring
B. Care giver
C. Cared for
D. Cared about

Set 2
A. Talkative
B. Quiet
C. Outgoing
D. Watcher

Set 4
A. Tired
B. Confused
C. Happy
D. Eager

PREPARATION AND ROOM SET-UP

Place all the "A" cards, "B" cards, "C" cards, and "D" cards together and face down.

Example:

Room Set-up

Have everyone stand.

STEP-BY-STEP WALK-THROUGH OF THE ACTIVITY

Step 1: Tell the participants that their assignment is to walk over to the sign that reflects the word that is most like them. They must select one. This is a forced-choice activity.

Step 2: Reveal the first set, saying: "Are you:

    A. Competitive?"

    B. Compromising?"

    C. Collaborative?"

    D. Accommodating?"

Step 3: Have individuals move to the sign that is most like them now. As they finish, walk up to each group and select one individual. Ask him or her to please share why he or she selected that particular word. Do this with each group no matter its size.

Step 4: Proceed with the second set. "Are you:

    A. Talkative?"

    B. Quiet?"

    C. Outgoing?"

    D. Watcher?"

Step 5: From where participants are currently, they should now move to the word that best describes them. Again, once they have positioned themselves, go to each group and select one individual. Have him or her share why he or she selected that particular word.

Step 6: Proceed to the third set. "Are you:

    A. Caring?"

    B. Care giver?"

    C. Cared for?"

    D. Cared about?"

Step 7: Repeat Step 5.

Step 8: Proceed to the fourth set. "Are you:

    A. Tired?"

    B. Confused?"

    C. Happy?"

    D. Eager?"

Step 9: Repeat Step 5.

Step 10: When finished, ask the participants to take their seats.

Step 11: Ask them, "What did we just do and why did we do it?" Let them tell you. It adds value to the activity. Typical responses include:

- Mixed up the groups

- Showed them they are similar in some ways, different in others

- Teams changed as assignment changed

Step 12: Add the following comments:
"Customer service is not a spectator sport. It takes a fully functional *independent* individual or 'I' to be a fully functional *interdependent* member of a team or 'We.'"

"The words you choose to go and stand by for whatever reasons reflected both your independent uniqueness and your shared beliefs as team members."

"By the way, they were all correct. There were no wrong words to respond to. They simply represented our differences and our similarities. That's normal; that's part of being a human being."

"Customer service people experience all of these and more in working with customers everyday. The key to success, of course, is to display the appropriate behavior/feeling/attitude at the appropriate time."

"We'll be talking more about what being a real team member means and what other characteristics/words/behaviors are needed to be effective as a team member."

Step 13: Thank everyone for their participation.

Notes, Insights, and Variations

■ You may wish to utilize this activity as a springboard to further work on effective teams. You may find the following definition useful.

Team Member: A person who deliberately sets out on a planned course of action designed to bring about the successful achievement of the team's goals. A team member is an individual who gives her or himself permission to contribute both independently and interdependently to the success of the team.

■ Have the participants add other words and characteristics they believe are essential to be an effective and efficient team member.

You've Got the Power 7

Activity Description

TIME GUIDELINE: 15 MINUTES (APPROXIMATE)

This simple, but powerful, activity is a wonderful way to encourage discussion and interaction among the participants by having them select the individual who will lead a discussion, answer the next question, be a team leader, etc.

Learning Objectives

PURPOSE:

This activity asks the participants to select someone from their peers who will have responsibility to perform any of a variety of tasks. It demonstrates how it helps to share the workload, spread leadership responsibilities, and get everyone involved.

PARTICIPANTS WILL BE ABLE TO:

Be involved in the decision-making process by selecting individuals for participation in a variety of activities.

BENEFITS:

Participants will benefit from the promotion of delegation and the sharing with peers.

Method of Instruction

MATERIALS NEEDED

Nerfball, soft stuffed animal, or other soft creative item

PREPARATION AND ROOM SET-UP

No additional preparation is required. This activity is applicable to whatever room set-up the presenter has selected.

STEP-BY-STEP WALK-THROUGH OF THE ACTIVITY

Step 1: Hold up the item you have selected (for the purpose of this discussion, we'll call it a ball) and say that it represents the power. Whoever is holding the ball has not only the ability but also the responsibility to lead.

Step 2: You select the first individual who will receive "the power," stating that when that person is finished with the task at hand, he or she may then select the next individual to whom to turn over "the power." It is that participant's choice and no one else's, because that individual has power. As you say this, throw the ball to the individual you have chosen.

Notes, Insights, and Variations

This is a fun activity that easily complements other activities. It can be used for review of portions of materials already covered, running through a list of questions with each individual with "the power" taking one of the questions, and so on. Be creative, have fun with it!

Call Centers and the Telephone

When a representative of your organization is on the phone with a customer, that individual represents all that your company stands for. For that particular customer, that customer service and/or sales representative is the company. The way the customer is treated at that moment can make all the difference in the world as to whether the business relationship continues or comes to a grinding halt. Even with a long-term customer where the relationship has taken perhaps years to develop, it can be destroyed in literally seconds should the customer not be treated properly. Is this important? To say the least, the telephone represents a critical vital link between the customer and your company. These activities reflect and support that vital link that must exist with each and every customer service occurrence.

Have You Ever Called You? 8

Activity Description

TIME GUIDELINE: 30 MINUTES

This activity is designed as a case study for the trainer to read aloud and then lead a discussion as to how each participant or each participant's organization would have handled it. The story is true, and in most cases, "we've all been there."

Learning Objectives

PURPOSE:

This activity will create discussion on how to promote good customer service.

PARTICIPANTS WILL BE ABLE TO:

1. Promote interaction among group members to discuss how the customer should have been treated.

2. Identify poor customer service and how it should have been avoided.

BENEFITS:

The activity encourages a sharing of identified poor customer service habits and provides a reminder that so many of us have experienced similar treatment. It allows for a creative sharing of what *should have happened* to provide proper customer service.

Method of Instruction

MATERIALS NEEDED

The Story of D.G. from Bland, Missouri

PREPARATION AND ROOM SET-UP

No additional preparation is required. This activity is applicable to whatever room set up the presenter has selected.

STEP-BY-STEP WALK-THROUGH OF THE ACTIVITY

Step 1: Read this story by D.G. from Bland, Missouri, aloud or have one of the participants read the story.

A letter to (blank) Department Store:

I placed a call to your 800 number and tried for 25 minutes to get someone to take my order for two quilts. Never could I get any person to speak to me. I heard your telephone menu at least five times while I tried unsuccessfully to press the button of my given choice. Over and over again the automated teller said, "Press or say number such and such and a representative will assist you" along with "if address change is wanted, if refund is wanted, stolen card, billing copy, etc." Pressing buttons got me nothing. The automated teller never stopped talking.

Discouraged, I called directly to your (blank) store. This service was worse than the automated service. Ten times an operator came on and told me to wait while she transferred my call. "Please hold, a representative will assist you momentarily." Each time I waited several minutes before once again a voice came on to tell me a representative would assist me momentarily.

Finally, a lady did answer. When I told her I was trying to buy two quilts, she asked: "For a lady or for a man?" I told her two quilts, domestic bedding, sheets, and pillow cases.

She said she would transfer me. Once more the voice came on with its "Please hold while I transfer your call."

Disgusted, I finally gave up. I had spent much time and long-distance telephone charges without service of any kind.

May I suggest you dial your store and listen to the traumatic service offered. I have been a customer of (blank) for many, many years. Never did I once believe that your service would deteriorate to this degree.

Step 2: Identify the poor customer service elements in the above story.

Step 3: Discuss how the customer should have been treated.

Step 4: Compare the participants' discussion with the response below.

The Telephone "Doctor"®'s Response:

At the start of every Telephone "Doctor"® program, I ask two questions:

The first question is: How many of you have a new employee orientation program on customer service and telephone skills? I'm always appalled by the lack of the show of hands.

The second question is: How many of you have ever called your company and asked for yourself, your service, or your product? Again, very few raise their hands.

So, the one assignment I give them all is to call up and ask for yourself, your service, or a product you offer. You cannot fix what you do not know. It is critically important to see yourself as others see you.

One time a lady asked me if they'd recognize her voice. They will, if you ask for someone else; but I promise you, when you call in and ask for yourself, they don't. I do it all the time. I call up and ask, "Is Nancy there?" And, trust me, no one has ever said, "Is that you playing around, Nancy?"

This person was kind enough to write to the store and tell them to call themselves. She gave them a thorough outline of what they could expect. Make the effort and a few times a month, call in and ask for yourself.

The Power 9
of Repetition

Activity Description

TIME GUIDELINE: 30 MINUTES

This activity is about doing the right things over and over again when it comes to delivering excellent customer service.

Learning Objectives

PURPOSE:

This activity demonstrates that there is power in the repetition of appropriate actions taken with customers.

PARTICIPANTS WILL BE ABLE TO:

1. Justify the repetition of action that reflects professionalism in customer service.

2. Identify particular behaviors and the benefits involved in their repetition.

BENEFITS:

There is a realization that positive, properly used repetition of action will get results and elicit responses that lead to successful outcomes with customers.

Method of Instruction

MATERIALS NEEDED

Flip chart
Markers

PREPARATION AND ROOM SET-UP

No additional preparation is required. This activity is applicable to whatever room set-up the presenter has selected.

STEP-BY-STEP WALK-THROUGH OF THE ACTIVITY

Step 1: Begin by saying,

"Most individuals relate repetition with boredom, monotony, and possibly even a lack of creativity. But, repetition can be a powerful tool in delivering excellent customer service; and when it produces the desired results, it certainly shows its worth."

Step 2: Then place participants in teams of four to five individuals and select a team leader for each group.

Step 3: (Activity 1) Ask participants to brainstorm and create a list of specific areas or actions taken within their customer service arena where repetition properly used (repetition of the right professional behavior) would be a powerful, positive, supportive force in building a customer-responsive relationship.

Allow 6 minutes for each team to brainstorm and create their lists. Then have each team leader or someone they have delegated share the ideas with the entire group. It's a good idea to write the responses on a flip chart and build a "master" list as this happens. Show appreciation for each team as they finish.

Step 4: (Activity 2) Let's take this a step further with the same teams and team leaders. Still focusing on the positive side of repetition that assists in focusing attention where it needs to be when it needs to be there, ask participants to create a second list, specifically as professional customer service people. What statements or phrases would they like to hear used on a regular basis when dealing with their customers? One example might be, "How may I help you?" Again, they have 6 minutes to create their list. When finished, have each team share their ideas; you may wish to place these on a flip chart as well.

Step 5: Then say,

"In conclusion, there is definitely a place for positive, properly used repetition of action that has been proven to get results and elicit responses that lead to successful outcomes with our customers."

Notes, Insights, and Variations

■ For Activity 1, here is an example of the type of responses you are looking for:

Have a greeting that one has committed to memory, one that identifies yourself, your company, perhaps your department or division, and lets the customer know that you are eager to assist them. Such as, good morning/afternoon. Thank you for calling (company name), this is (your name), how may I help you?

■ Responses using this format of repetition should be stated sincerely, enthusiastically, and with feeling and care. Do not come across in a monotone or robotic manner or the purpose for which this tool is intended is defeated.

■ Possible responses for Activity 2:

__ How may I help you?

__ Yes, we can!

__ Thank you for the order.

__ I appreciate your business.

__ Is there anything else I can help you with today?

__ Please . . .

__ We certainly look forward to doing business with you in the future.

Calling Your Own Company 10

Activity Description

TIME GUIDELINE: 30 MINUTES

In this activity, participants actually call their own companies, preferably own work stations to leave a specific message. It is a great way to listen and evaluate one's own voice and message.

Learning Objectives

PURPOSE:

This activity will allow for a self-evaluation of telephone techniques, particularly focusing on the content of the message and the manner in which it is delivered.

PARTICIPANTS WILL BE ABLE TO:

1. Evaluate their own telephone techniques.

2. Identify areas of strengths.

3. Identify areas needing improvements and specific actions that it takes to do so.

BENEFITS:

Participants have the opportunity to listen to their own voice and the words they use in the message that is left. It provides a wonderful self-evaluation of not only the content of their message but how that message is being delivered.

Method of Instruction

MATERIALS NEEDED

Telephone stations

PREPARATION AND ROOM SET-UP

Allow participants 15 minutes to prepare for the activity after it is explained.

STEP-BY-STEP WALK-THROUGH OF THE ACTIVITY

Step 1: Discussion

> Whenever you use the telephone, you are the voice of your company. You represent everything your company stands for; and in the mind of the customer, you are the company. When your voice is warm and friendly and when you are courteous and tactful, customers will enjoy dealing with you. A customer-responsive relationship can take years to develop, and it can be destroyed in seconds, totally dependent on your contact, your treatment, your interaction and professionalism or lack thereof with the customer.

Step 2: Call to workplace

> Each participants should prepare to call his or her own workplace, where you will be leaving a message for yourself.

Step 3: Criteria to follow

> A. Act as if you are not calling yourself but rather a customer.
>
> B. Describe what your company does—the services you provide, the product you sell.

C. Identify the needs you fulfill for your customer.

D. Identify what solutions you provide.

Note: It's critical that each participant be able to provide the information above. If we don't educate the customer to the value we bring, how we are different from the competition, and the quality of our services and products, who will?

Step 4: Meet with individuals before the call to discuss their presentation and encourage their professionalism.

Step 5: Have each individual make the call.

Step 6: Evaluation and action plan

At some point in time, either as part of a follow-up activity or during the session, evaluate those messages that were recorded at the meeting according to the following criteria:

A. Did you properly identify yourself and your company?

B. Could you understand yourself (proper articulation, rate of speaking, etc.)?

C. Were you able to describe what your company does with clarity of understanding and confidence?

D. Did you describe your company's products and services?

E. Did you properly educate the customer to the value/quality/why your company is unique?

F. Other observations?

■ What other items did you become aware of as you listened to your message that would improve your communication and telephone techniques?

■ What specific actions will you take to make this happen?

Notes, Insights, and Variations

If setting up arrangements to call their own offices is too difficult to arrange, this activity can be done right at the session by simply having each individual's message recorded right in class (we recommend they be isolated during the recording). The remaining activities can be implemented as classroom activities or incorporated into a follow-up assignment.

Evaluating Self 11

Activity Description

TIME GUIDELINE: 15–30 MINUTES

Periodically it can be very beneficial to stop and take a look at where you are, what you are doing, and how you are using your telephone skills. This activity is a *focus on self* regarding one's telephone techniques.

Learning Objectives

PURPOSE:

This activity raises participants to a higher level of awareness about their telephone performance level as customer service representatives.

PARTICIPANTS WILL BE ABLE TO:

Perform a self-evaluation of their telephone techniques.

BENEFITS:

A periodic self-evaluation raises individual awareness and focuses on the level of service being provided to the customer.

Method of Instruction

MATERIALS NEEDED

Handout 11.1: Self-Evaluation: Telephone Techniques

PREPARATION AND ROOM SET-UP

No additional preparation is required. This activity is applicable to whatever room set-up the presenter has selected.

STEP-BY-STEP WALK-THROUGH OF THE ACTIVITY

Step 1: As a group, take a moment to identify the use of the telephone. Then, periodically, evaluate your own use of that vital link between you and your customer.

Item 1: *Do I answer calls correctly by identifying my company, myself, and the customer?*

You should have a pat response that you give to your customers. It tells the customer you are ready to take care of their needs. It lets them know they have called the right place and exactly who they are speaking with. You're ready for business to commence.

Item 2: *Do I listen to the customer's message with complete attention?*

It takes a great deal more effort to listen than to hear. Listening is focusing your attention where it needs to be when it needs to be there.

Item 3: *Do I ask questions that cause the customer to think and share more information with me?*

These are often referred to as exploratory questions. Questions that probe the mind of the customer cause the customer to think and respond by talking more, so that, in turn, we can listen more.

Item 4: *Do I respond in a caring manner to the customer's comments, questions, and concerns?*

The old cliché, "Your customers don't care about how much you know until they know how much you care" holds true. Caring is one of your major building blocks in the foundation of a customer-responsive relationship.

Item 5: *Do I keep the conversation from wandering and take responsibility for bringing it back to business tactfully?*

The responsibility is on your shoulders to keep focused on the business at hand. It's nice to socialize and chit chat, but there is work to be done. Behind this customer is another, and behind that one, another, and so on. Be tactful and polite as you bring the conversation back to business.

Item 6: *If I have to place the customer on hold, do I do it properly?*

Whenever possible, give the customer a choice. It helps them to feel in control.

- May I please put you on hold (and wait for the response)?

or

- May I take your name and number and I'll call you back (be certain that you do)?

or

- May I have someone else help you?

or

- If they are asking for someone else and that individual is not available, say, May I help you?

Item 7: *Do I maintain a pleasant tone of voice throughout the conversation?*

Your tone of voice has a major impact on the message you are delivering. You may be using the most beautiful words in your message, but if it is not backed by a supportive, caring tone of voice, it will not be received well.

Item 8: *Am I courteous to the customer throughout the conversation?*

Treat the customer with the same dignity and respect you would like to receive.

Item 9: *Do I demonstrate enthusiasm and self-confidence to the customer?*

Enthusiasm has its roots in the ancient Greek language. It literally means "the spirit within." Enthusiasm is contagious and can impact those around you in a positive manner.

Item 10: *Did I take notes?*

Don't leave details to memory. Get all the facts and avoid having to go back and do it again.

Item 11: *Did I use feelings to express an idea or a mood?*

A monotone, robotic voice like HAL the computer from *2001: A Space Odyssey* can drive people up a wall. Demonstrate that they are speaking with a healthy, alive, caring human being and not some machine.

Item 12: *Was the rate of my speaking proper?*

Right around 150 wpm is the average rate found to be received well. The communication process requires two individuals working to understand each other. Contribute as much as possible to the process.

Item 13: *When speaking on the phone, do I avoid chewing gum or eating? Do I enunciate so that the customer understands me and I do not have to repeat items back to the customer?*

You may have the greatest ideas and messages to give your customer; but, if they can't understand you as a result of some obstacle to effective speech you've placed in your mouth, something's wrong.

Item 14: *Do I have a smile in my voice that the customer can visualize or feel?*

Most people believe that a smile permeates right through that phone line. A smile adds greatly to your face value.

Item 15: *Did I fulfill the customer's needs? Did I provide a solution?*

This is what it's all about. This is the business we are in—the needs fulfillment business.

Item 16: *Did I ask for the order?*

> We always like to end with this one because it provides closure to all the hard work that proceeded it. Nothing happens until somebody sells something— and we always like to add—for a profit.

Items 17–20: *Other important evaluation questions with which I am concerned:*

> Four spaces are provided to personalize your evaluation even more.

Step 2: Using Handout 11.1, have the participants evaluate their own telephone techniques.

Notes, Insights, and Variations

This is a great activity to complement and support any telephone training. It is a particularly good review toward the end of a program and a good follow-up tool.

Self-Evaluation: Telephone Techniques

Please review the following periodically to fine-tune skills as a professional customer service representative.

1. Do I answer calls correctly? Do I identify my company, myself, and the customer?

2. Do I listen to the customer's message with complete attention?

3. Do I ask questions that cause the customer to think and share more information with me?

4. Do I respond in a caring manner to the customer's comments, questions, and concerns?

5. Do I keep the conversation from wandering and take responsibility for bringing it back to business tactfully?

6. If I have to place the customer on hold, do I do it properly?

7. Do I maintain a pleasant tone of voice throughout the conversation?

8. Am I courteous to the customer throughout the conversation?

9. Do I demonstrate enthusiasm and self-confidence to the customer?

10. Did I take notes?

11. Did I use feelings to express an idea or a mood?

12. Was the rate of my speaking proper?

13. When speaking on the phone, do I avoid chewing gum or eating? Do I enunciate so that the customer understands me and I do not have to repeat items back to the customer?

SELF-EVALUATION: TELEPHONE TECHNIQUES (CONTINUED)

14. Do I have a smile in my voice that the customer can visualize or feel?

15. Did I fulfill the customer's needs? Did I provide a solution?

16. Did I ask for the order?

Other important evaluation questions I am concerned with:

17. _____

_____

_____

_____

18. _____

_____

_____

_____

19. _____

_____

_____

_____

20. _____

_____

_____

_____

Professionalism with No Excuses

Our customers want service, expect it, and demand it. Any other response, action, or behavior is usually summed up in the mind of the customer by one word, **excuse.**

In the world of survivors, for those who will persevere and achieve the next level of success, the word *excuse* does not exist. There are only results, actions, and solutions. A true professional is constantly adjusting, learning, accepting challenges, and creatively building a customer-responsive relationship. These activities reflect that challenge of remaining a professional under often adverse conditions with no excuses, just service.

Excuses, Excuses, Excuses 12

Activity Description

TIME GUIDELINE: 20 MINUTES

This activity promotes group discussion to tap the creative professionalism of each individual. It awakens the realization that no excuses should be given for not providing excellent service.

Learning Objectives

PURPOSE:

Attendees will have the realization that customers want, need, and expect excellent service with no excuses.

PARTICIPANTS WILL BE ABLE TO:

1. Conclude that there are no excuses for not delivering excellent customer service.

2. Determine that creativity is a critical tool in responding professionally to customers.

3. Evaluate actual situations in which excuses have been given and determine what should have happened.

BENEFITS:

This is a great activity to get the creative juices flowing and to realize that there should not be any excuses for not delivering excellent customer service.

Method of Instruction

MATERIALS NEEDED

Handout 12.1: Excuses, Excuses, Excuses

PREPARATION AND ROOM SET-UP

No additional preparation is required. This activity is applicable to whatever room set-up the presenter has selected.

STEP-BY-STEP WALK-THROUGH OF THE ACTIVITY

Step 1: Place participants in teams of four to six individuals, and select team leaders.

Step 2: Distribute Handout 12.1. Explain that each team will share one handout and list three to five common excuses they have either heard other customer service representatives give or they themselves have used for offering indifferent or poor customer service.

Examples: My computer is down.

I'm having a Monday.

That's not my customer!

I just took the last call!

Step 3: Tell participants,

"Comments such as these bring service to a screeching halt. Now, please be aware that the most important part of this activity is not the excuses you come up with. The most critical part is the second column titled, 'What should have happened?' What should have happened instead of that excuse ever being said? What should have happened to give the customer the service they expect, want, and need?

"This is where your creativity as professionals really needs to be utilized. For example, when someone realizes that their computer is down, does that mean that business comes to a halt and we simply lose that customer? Or, can we creatively come up with other solutions and actions to, at the very best, keep the door open for future business?"

Step 4: Have the team leaders lead their groups in a discussion using the handout as a guideline. Emphasize again that the most critical part of the assignment is the second column—what should have happened?

Step 5: Allow 10 minutes for discussion. Then, have each group share one item at a time—the excuse and what should have happened.

Notes, Insights, and Variations

You may wish to obtain a copy of our book, *EXCUSES, EXCUSES, EXCUSES . . . For Not Delivering Excellent Customer Service—And What Should Happen!* (HRD Press, 2001). It contains 117 excuses that have been given for offering the type of service our customers do not want. It then takes that inappropriate behavior to the next level of what should have happened. It is a wonderful tool to complement and support not only this activity but any training for customer service.

Excuses, Excuses, Excuses

List five common excuses you hear customer service representatives give for offering indifferent or poor customer service.

Excuse #1   What should have happened?

_____   _____
_____   _____
_____   _____

Excuse #2   What should have happened?

_____   _____
_____   _____
_____   _____

Excuse #3   What should have happened?

_____   _____
_____   _____
_____   _____

Excuse #4   What should have happened?

_____   _____
_____   _____
_____   _____

Excuse #5   What should have happened?

_____   _____
_____   _____
_____   _____

Make It a Miracle 13

Activity Description

TIME GUIDELINE: 15 MINUTES

This activity involves a slight-of-hand demonstration to show how the customer's perception of reality is what really counts.

Learning Objectives

PURPOSE:

This activity demonstrates the power of perception and the image we place in the mind of the customer regarding our organization and our services.

PARTICIPANTS WILL BE ABLE TO:

Observe how a customer's perception can be different from their perception.

BENEFITS:

This activity illustrates that the customer's perception of reality and of the level of service received is critical to an organization's success.

Method of Instruction

MATERIALS NEEDED

Overhead 13.1: Make It A Miracle
One blank flip chart
One two-ply tissue
One volunteer (preferably someone who is a little shorter than you are and
   good natured)

PREPARATION AND ROOM SET-UP

No additional preparation is required. This activity is applicable to whatever room set-up
   the presenter has selected (position one flip chart at the front of the room).

STEP-BY-STEP WALK-THROUGH OF THE ACTIVITY

Step 1: Show the overhead.

Step 2: Tell participants,

"I love that word **MIRACLE**—*Make It Really A Colossal Learning Experience.*
And, I'd like to compare, if I may, what you do to watching a play."

"You know that when you go to watch and enjoy a play, you are the
customer. You have certain expectations. You expect the actors to know their
lines, be properly attired in their costumes, move about the stage properly,
and give a professional performance. You expect to see a miracle."

"Now, think of your own work environment, if you will. When your customer
enters your establishment (or calls on the phone), they expect to see and hear
a MIRACLE also. They expect a smooth-running machine of an organization.
They expect caring, courteous, and knowledgeable customer service
representatives who are enthusiastic, ready to help, and not only able to get
along with them, but with each other as well. Again, they expect a MIRACLE—
every time—Make It Really A Colossal Learning Experience."

"Now, let's go back to the play. What's going on backstage is quite different
from what the customers in the seats are viewing and experiencing. The

customers are seeing that miracle we spoke of, but backstage is something very different—something I like to call 'organized chaos.' You have individuals moving props about to the appropriate location, actors scurrying about making costume changes or finding their mark for their entry to the stage, and crew members assisting in a variety of ways. A great deal of activity that is absolutely necessary to occur behind the scenes but not at all necessary or expected for viewing or listening to by those in the seats who are watching the miracle—the customers."

"Now, within your organization, do you have 'organized chaos'? Of course you do. Is it necessary? For the most part, yes it is. But is it something the customer needs to hear or to see? No! The customer needs and expects to see that miracle."

Step 3: At this point, call the volunteer to the front of the room, and thank the participant for assisting you. You should have your two-ply tissue (slightly pulled apart in advance so as not to hinder your demonstration) on a table or standing near you. Announce that he or she is going to be the customer and will stand with his or her back to the flip chart facing the fellow associates.

Step 4: Lift up the tissue saying, "You know I love when you take a tissue and then pull it apart and then you have the kleeneye (old vaudeville humor)." Actually separate the two-ply tissue as you say this.

Step 5: Point at the overhead with MIRACLE on it. Say,

"This is what we want the customer to see. We want to "Make It Really a Colossal Learning Experience" every time they do business with us. Now, this tissue *(hold the tissue in your left hand showing it to the others in the room and to your volunteer)* represents that organized chaos we spoke of. It's alright for us to see it, but the customer does not need to see it or experience it."

Step 6: Stand slightly to the right of and slightly ahead of your volunteer as you say:

"The customer does not need to see it or experience it." Crumple the tissue up with both hands, rolling it into a small ball and covering it in your hand.

Say again as you open your hands revealing the tissue, that "This organized chaos is necessary; you can almost feel it and grasp it, but the customer does not need it at all."

Step 7: Now comes the slight of hand. What you are going to do is crumple up the tissue with your two hands together, moving the tissue to your right hand. As you are saying, "We all have our organized chaos; we all have our ups and downs," move your arms up and down in front of your volunteer. Your hands should go up and down in front of them at least two times. Now, here is the key. Be certain when you raise your hands, holding the tissue, that you go above his or her head. The very first time you do this with the tissue in your right hand, toss it over the volunteer and the flip chart. Keep your hands together, moving your hands up and down one or two more times.

Note: The reason why you must toss the tissue the first time is that your volunteer will start to follow your hands more closely the second and third times, so you must get rid of the tissue the first time.

As you bring your arms down the final time with your hands still together, you are saying, "Our customer does not want or need to see the organized chaos. They need to see the miracle." As you are stating this, slowly open your hand right in front of your volunteer.

Step 8: The audience response tells it all. Because if you have done the activity successfully, they will see the wide-eyed expression of your volunteer wondering where the tissue went and this will cause some laughter.

Step 9: Show appreciation to the volunteer and mention that even though this is just a very simple little activity, it demonstrates a key point. The perception of the customers of our service is critical. We need to show them a MIRACLE every time they do business with us.

Notes, Insights, and Variations

■ Practice makes perfect. Try this with friends and family before your first real attempt. It's much easier than it sounds.

■ After you reveal that the first tissue is gone and the volunteer doesn't have a clue as to where it went, you may want to repeat the entire process with the other half of the tissue. Keep it handy after you separated the two plies. One time we even threw the entire box of tissue over the individual's head. It makes for an entertaining activity, but also gets a powerful message across.

Have fun with it! It's a great activity to do just prior to a break.

Make It A Miracle

M — Make

I — It

R — Really

A — A

C — Colossal

L — Learning

E — Experience

Overcoming Obstacles **14**

Activity Description

TIME GUIDELINE: 40 MINUTES

This activity focuses on our inherent responsibilities as professionals to accept challenges, overcome those hurdles the customer places before us, and achieve success by providing services and fulfilling needs.

Learning Objectives

PURPOSE:

The purpose of this activity is to identify the obstacles to excellent customer service and the specific actions necessary to overcome those obstacles.

PARTICIPANTS WILL BE ABLE TO:

1. Recognize that problems and challenges must be faced and overcome to achieve success with our customers.

2. Determine specific actions one must be prepared for to provide solutions and fulfill needs.

BENEFITS:

This activity allows the group to bring concerns, obstacles, and barriers to success to the surface, realizing that others share similar feelings and confrontations, and that these obstacles are normal and allow us to focus our energy on solutions.

Method of Instruction

MATERIALS NEEDED

Handout 14.1: Story: The Greatest Hurdler
Flip chart
Markers

PREPARATION AND ROOM SET-UP

No additional preparation is required. This activity is applicable to whatever room set-up the presenter has selected.

STEP-BY-STEP WALK-THROUGH OF THE ACTIVITY

Step 1: Divide participants into groups and select team leaders. Each team should discuss the following items and be prepared to share its results (8 minutes).

■ What items can you identify that represent obstacles to excellent customer service, internally and externally?

■ For each item listed, come up with at least one action that would correct or eliminate the problem.

Step 2: When finished, each team reports its result to the entire group.

Step 3: List these items on a flip chart with input from the entire group. Focus on solutions and improvements.

Notes, Insights, and Variations

Attaining our goals and achieving the next level of success with our customers is a tremendous challenge facing us all.

Story: The Greatest Hurdler

A group of high school coaches are standing outside on the school grounds in front of the gym. A tenth-grade boy (Nick), full of enthusiasm, is out running with the track team. As he passes this group of coaches, Nick yells out, "I'm going to be the greatest hurdler in the history of our school." The coaches smile, and Nick runs on. On his second trip around the building, he meets up with the coaches, and once again proclaims, "I'm going to be the greatest hurdler in the history of our school." This time Nick has captured the attention of one of the coaches; as he comes around the building a third time, the coach steps out and stops him. The coach asks Nick, "Nick, how are you going to become the greatest hurdler in the history of our school?" Nick steps back, startled at the coach's question. He looks around as if protecting something and asks the coach, "Do you really want to know the secret?" The coach says, "Yes, I do, Nick. How are you going to be the greatest hurdler in the history of the school?"

Nick motions for the coach to come closer, and looks around the area again as if to make certain it is secure. The coach looks around also. Nick motions once more for the coach to come even closer, and whispers in the coach's ear, "If you want to become the greatest hurdler in the history of the school, you go for the tape. You don't go for the hurdle; you go for the tape." (Say this softly two times. Then say it loudly.) "You go for the tape; you don't go for the hurdle—you go for the tape!"

What words of wisdom coming from this young man, a tenth grader! Sure, we are all going to have hurdles and obstacles to overcome; but if you set your sights on the goal, if you're focused on your vision, you are going to get there.

The Rules Have 15
Changed the Game

Activity Description

TIME GUIDELINE: 45 MINUTES

True professionals understand the rules of the game they are playing and how results will be impacted when those rules change. This powerful activity illustrates that perhaps things are not as simple as they seem to be, and that we need to be flexible to the needs of our customers to get results.

Learning Objectives

PURPOSE:

This activity demonstrates the importance of operating under the proper rules, guidelines, or processes to obtain desired results.

PARTICIPANTS WILL BE ABLE TO:

1. Understand the need to be flexible to our customers' needs.

2. Determine that inflexibility often produces poor results.

3. Differentiate between reacting and responding to our customers' needs.

BENEFITS:

Participants must respond to our customers' needs and not simply react to them. Responding takes thought and understanding to ensure that the actions taken are appropriate and will produce the desired results.

Method of Instruction

MATERIALS NEEDED

A plastic bottle (to represent your customer)
A ping-pong ball (to represent your customer's needs)
Table
Strip of masking tape placed on floor, 10 feet from the table
Flip chart
Cassette with marching music

PREPARATION AND ROOM SET-UP

See the diagram for placement of the masking tape and the table arrangement for the activity.
No additional preparation is required. This activity is applicable to whatever room set-up the presenter has selected.
Write the rules below on the flip chart in advance.

Rules:

1. Stand on the strip of tape (on the floor).

2. Extend your right arm out with the elbow locked.

3. Your objective is to hit the ball off the bottle using only your middle finger (demonstrate). One flick only per person.

4. Remain upright as you walk by.

5. Do not rotate your arm or wrist side to side. Up and down movement of the arm is okay.

STEP-BY-STEP WALK-THROUGH OF THE ACTIVITY

Step 1: Tell participants,

"This is a powerful activity—something that up front seems so easy to accomplish, yet so many fail. It's a lesson in being certain that you are operating under the right set of rules as you deal with and deliver excellent service to your customers."

"The objective of this game is to demonstrate the point of knowing the appropriate rules in order to 'play the game' of customer service and fulfill your customer's needs. What I have here is an ordinary plastic bottle, which represents 'Your Customer.'"

Step 2: Hand the bottle to a participant for examination, and then place it at the appropriate spot for the activity (see Figure 15.1.). Place the ping-pong ball, which represents "Your Customer's Needs" on top of the bottle.

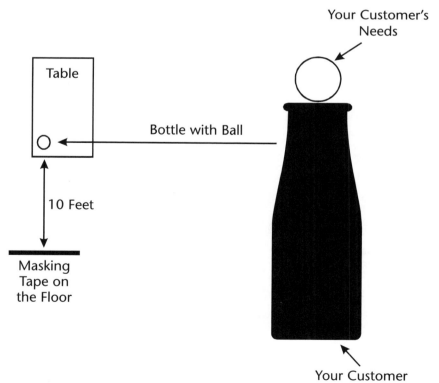

Figure 15.1 The Rules Have Changed Game

Step 3: Then, say,

"Your goal is to fulfill your customer's needs. Now, the only way you are able to do that is by hitting the ping-pong ball off the bottle. You only get one chance at it. Sounds easy enough, doesn't it? However, to play this game you must play by my rules—not yours."

Step 4: Review the rules on the flip chart. "Remember, you must hit the ball in order to fulfill your customer's needs. If you hit the entire bottle or knock it over or miss, you have caused irreparable damage to your customer."

Step 5: Have all participants line up with the first player on the tape. Each player will follow right behind the other. *Note:* Ask the first participant to assist in retrieving the ball as each person hits it off the bottle.

Step 6: Then, say,

"Now, I want you to move along at a rather fast pace and return right back to your seat, almost at a marching pace. I happen to have some marching music."

Step 7: Put on the music, clap hands/march/etc. Tell the players to observe each other to be certain that the rules are being followed. Stand next to the tape and check that each individual is getting off to a proper start, elbow locked, hand held appropriately. Note: If you have a left-handed player, move the bottle to the opposite side of the table. Keep the line moving.

Step 8: After the game has been played, review the results.

"If the rules were followed, no one should have hit the ball. Why? Because as you approach the bottle, your arm and hand move in alignment with your target (the ball). As you line up, you cannot see the ball because it is blocked from your view by your own hand. You might not have noticed this because of the pace at which you were traveling. That's why we used the marching music."

Notes, Insights, and Variations

Divide the group into teams and appoint a spokesperson for each. Give each team 4 minutes to discuss what this activity has to do with sales and fulfilling customers' needs. Possible comments—choose those that fit your group's experience:

- Remember that definition of insanity . . . doing the same thing over and over and over again and expecting different results? It's not going to happen.

- You may be trying very hard, but if you're not operating under the appropriate rules or guidelines, you may never fulfill your customer's needs.

- Remember, this is a very easy "common sense" task to accomplish (hitting the ball off the bottle) if you're doing it according to the appropriate rules. You need to adjust and adapt your behavior for each customer.

- The more you know your customer, the more prepared you will be to deal with situations as they present themselves, and respond rather than react. So, if you are not identifying problems and challenges that must be faced and then responding appropriately to them, you may never fulfill your customer's needs, no matter how hard you feel you are trying.

Defining Spectacular Service: How We Impact Our Customers Every Day 16

Activity Description

TIME GUIDELINE: 45 MINUTES

This activity gives participants an opportunity to develop a shared definition of what makes spectacular service.

Learning Objectives

PURPOSE:

The development of a shared definition of what makes spectacular service by those who deliver service every day.

PARTICIPANTS WILL BE ABLE TO:

1. Define what is meant by spectacular service.

2. Identify some key characteristics and components of spectacular service.

3. Explore the three service differentiators that separate one company from another.

4. Discuss the two sides of the service delivery equation.

BENEFITS:

Participants will achieve an agreed-upon definition of spectacular service. Those who deliver service everyday are in a position to determine and identify key components of that service.

Method of Instruction

MATERIALS NEEDED

Handout 16.1: Spectacular Customer Service Word Map
Overhead 16.1: Key Differentiators
Overhead 16.2: Two Sides to Service
Flip chart
Markers

PREPARATION AND ROOM SET-UP

This activity is designed for a classroom layout with a facilitator. Participants are divided into small groups that will define spectacular service, create a word map, and present their definitions to the entire group.
Photocopy the Spectacular Customer Service Word Map.
Prepare the overheads.

STEP-BY-STEP WALK-THROUGH OF THE ACTIVITY

Step 1: Word Map Group Activity

Introduce the activity. Tell the participants:

■ From the previous activity it is clear that everyone in the group has a lot of ideas about what goes into spectacular service.

■ Because we all frequently have the opportunity to be customers, we usually think we know good service (and poor service) when we see it.

■ That really is only one perspective, however. The people in the best position to talk about all the qualities of spectacular service are those who not only receive service but those who provide it every day as well. They really are in the best position to describe what it means to give good service.

- Participants fall into that category because they are actively providing service every day.

- This activity will give them an opportunity to develop a shared definition of what makes up spectacular service.

Step 2: Divide the participants into small groups or let them work in their "table" groups.

Step 3: Distribute Handout 16.1 to each participant.

Step 4: Distribute a blank flip chart page and markers to each team.

Step 5: Tell teams to appoint a reporter and a recorder. The recorder will prepare the group's presentation (definition of service), and the reporter will give the presentation to the larger group.

Step 6: Tell participants,

- You will now have the opportunity to work in your groups for about 7 to 9 minutes to create a shared definition of spectacular customer service.

- I have given you a worksheet organizer to help generate some creative thinking.

- The word map is simply a series of spaces where you can enter statements, adjectives, examples, and other descriptors of service.

Step 7: Describe the use of the word map:

- The word map is not linear; you are encouraged to jump around when you use it.

- The word map is just an aid to help teams develop a definition of service.

- You use the word map by jotting down answers to the questions listed.

  "What is it?" In the left-hand boxes, write what you think high-quality or "spectacular" customer service really is. In the three spaces at the bottom of the page, write some examples of spectacular service.

In the right-hand column, write metaphors or similes that help you define service, e.g., "Giving good service is like being on a winning basketball team; everyone does their part."

■ After your group has used the word map and discussed the issue for a few minutes, you should come up with a shared and agreed-upon description or definition of spectacular service and post that description to your chart page.

Step 8: Group Presentations—Definitions of Spectacular Service (25 minutes)

Allow groups to work for 7 to 9 minutes. At the end of that time, reconvene the large group and ask the reporters from each of the groups to present their definition of spectacular service. Tell participants that their definitions of service should be appropriate for both internal and external customers.

Step 9: During the group presentations, write and post any key words and concepts that appear repeatedly within the definitions and presentations of different small groups.

Step 10: Following each small group presentation, build on and draw out discussion about the following key concepts:

■ Attitude and enthusiasm

■ Knowledge

■ Care, concern, and courtesy

■ Responsiveness

■ Reliability

■ Skill and expertise

■ Helpfulness—going the extra mile

Step 11: Post the flip chart pages containing the definitions each group developed. Ask participants to select the one or two definitions they feel are most comprehensive in describing all aspects of spectacular service. Provide a small reward to the members of the winning team (or teams).

Step 12: Debrief the small group presentations. (15 minutes)

Ask participants: "Which is more important when serving and trying to satisfy customers, product or the person? Which has a more important role, the product or service purchased by the customer or the people involved in delivering and providing the product or service?"

Answer: Help participants understand that while there is no clear cut right or wrong answer to this question, the product plays a smaller role than the person delivering the product and helping with the buying and/or customer service process. If a customer purchases a wonderful product but has a bad experience, he or she will not remember all the good things about the product, only the bad experience. On the other hand, if the customer purchases a poor product but the people are really helpful and understanding in the process, the customer will be less upset about the product. Give examples as necessary.

Step 13: During the debrief discussion, ensure that these key points surface:

■ The "service" a company provides is different from the "services" it provides. A cleaning organization provides the service of cleaning your home or office; the manner in which they do the cleaning (e.g., thoroughly, on a timely basis, courteously, unobtrusively) refers to their level of service.

■ Service means adding people to the product (in the earlier example, if the office cleaning is the product, then the way the office is cleaned is really the service portion of the equation.)

■ The importance of service is demonstrated every day; patients in a doctor's or dentist's office want more than just treatment, hotel guests want more than just a room, restaurant patrons want more than just a meal.

Step 14: Show Overhead 16.1

Display the overhead and briefly review the things that differentiate one organization from another, using this discussion to emphasize the importance of people and the service they provide as essential to an organization's success. Tell participants that this fact has placed pressure on all organizations to be better, faster, or different in the way in which they provide service to their customers.

Step 15: Show Overhead 16.2

Display the overhead and briefly review the importance of the process and people sides of the service delivery equation. Tell participants that there are really two important components to an organization's and an individual's ability to deliver spectacular service. When providing spectacular service, they are to focus on two factors:

- The procedural side of service, which consists of the systems and procedures used to deliver the product or service.

- The personal side of service; how service personnel (using their attitudes, behaviors, and verbal skills) interact with customers.

Ask participants which of the two factors they can influence the most.

Answer: The personal side, because they have direct and immediate control over this factor, while the influence they have over the procedural side is actually shared with the organization.

Step 16: Recap the definition activity by emphasizing that however you define spectacular service, it involves identifying what the customer needs and wants and then meeting those needs in a prompt and courteous fashion.

Notes, Insights, and Variations

We have a lot of ideas about what goes into spectacular service. Since we all frequently have the opportunity to be customers, we usually think we know good service (and poor service) when we see it. However, that really is only one perspective. The people in the best position to talk about all the qualities of spectacular service are those who not only receive service, but those who provide it everyday as well. Participants fall into that category because they are actively providing service everyday.

Spectacular Customer Service Word Map

What Is It?

What Is It Like?

What Are Some Examples?

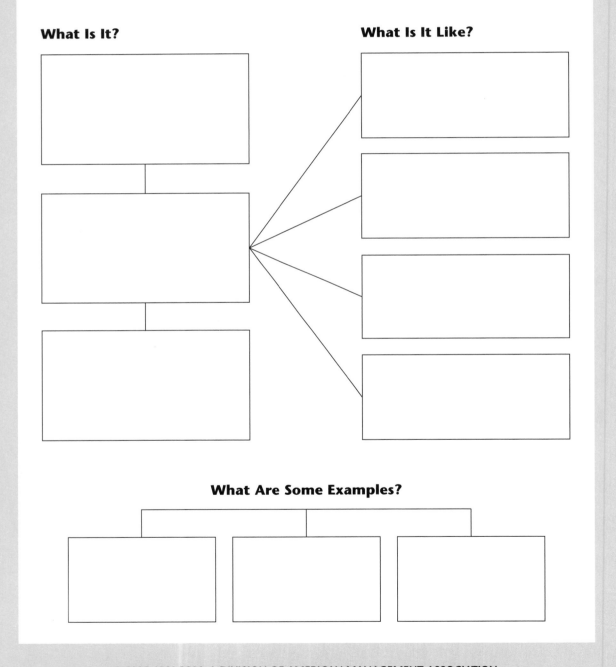

Key Differentiators

There are three things that distinguish or separate organizations from one another:

1. The product or service they provide and the price of that product or service.

2. The quality of the product or professional service.

3. The type of service they provide (the way they do business with their customers).

Two Sides to Service

■ Procedural: The systems and procedures used to deliver products and/or services.

■ Personal: How service personnel (using their attitudes, behaviors, and verbal skills) interact with customers.

Communication: Listening to Your Customers

Communication is the magic of transforming thought into vivid experience that humans can both express and understand, not just in language, but in signs and symbols and gestures—and in facial expressions that color the message with humanness and warmth, with stimulation, with understanding, with quality, with vitality, with friendship, and with sharing.

It is said that the greatest courtesy you can give to another human being is to listen to them. How can we possibly even begin to resolve our customers' problems or fulfill their needs if we do not begin by listening? And, even that is not enough; for often getting the customer to talk so that we can listen is like pulling teeth. So, in addition to listening, we must be able to probe the mind of the customer and get them to talk even more by asking the right questions so that, in turn, we can listen even more. Only then can we truly arrive at the proper understanding of what the customer actually desires and act accordingly.

These activities demonstrate the power of active listening techniques and the importance of utilizing every tool we have for the best results.

Active Versus Passive Communication 17

Activity Description

TIME GUIDELINE: 45 MINUTES

This activity demonstrates the difference between active (two-way) communication and passive (one-way) communication. It allows the participants to arrive at their own conclusions regarding the use and application of both forms of communication.

Learning Objectives

PURPOSE:

The purpose of this activity is to illustrate that a true professional utilizes both passive and active communication to achieve clarity of understanding.

PARTICIPANTS WILL BE ABLE TO:

1. Identify the components of passive (one-way) communication.

2. Identify the components of active (two-way) communication.

3. Determine the value of both passive and active communication and when it is best to utilize each one.

BENEFITS:

Participants will achieve the realization that a true professional uses both passive and active communication.

Method of Instruction

MATERIALS NEEDED

Handout 17.1: Story
Flip chart, overhead transparency, or computer with PowerPoint capabilities

PREPARATION AND ROOM SET-UP

No additional preparation is required. The activity is applicable to whatever room set-up the presenter has selected.

STEP-BY-STEP WALK-THROUGH OF THE ACTIVITY

Step 1: Select three individuals and have them wait outside the room where they cannot hear the introductory comments for the activity. Explain what is going to happen to the entire group.

Step 2: Say,

"We are going to demonstrate the difference between passive (one-way) communication and active (two-way) communication."

Note: It is recommended that you place these terms either on a flip chart, overhead transparency, or PowerPoint presentation as you review them.

Step 3: Tell participants,

"With passive communication all you can do is listen. You may not ask questions. You may not paraphrase or summarize. You cannot have anything repeated. All you can do is listen. Now, fortunately, there are not too many circumstances that present themselves in which this is your only option. The sad reality is that too often individuals allow themselves only to practice passive communication, ending in poor, often tragic results.

"Now, with active (two-way) communication, not only do you have the opportunity, in fact you are expected, to ask questions, repeat, paraphrase, summarize, verify, whatever it takes to be certain that you have achieved understanding, that you and your customer are in fact both heading in the same direction."

Step 4: Now, ask the three individuals you have selected to go to the designated area outside the room where they cannot hear you. Distribute Handout 17.1 and explain to the others: "I will read the following story to the first individual called in."

Step 5: Hand out a copy of the story to the observers. Read the story to the group (see Handout 17.1).

Step 6: Say, "I will only read the story only once. Nothing can be repeated and no questions can be answered, nothing summarized, and nothing paraphrased. This is an example of passive listening."

Step 7: Call in the first person and read the story. After you have read the story, say,

"Now would you please retell the story to these good people. Please include a beginning, a middle, and an end."

Step 8: Have the first individual remain standing with you as you call in the second individual. Again, explain the situation to the person, but add that the first person is going to tell him or her a story. The first person can only tell it once—no questions, no paraphrasing, etc. All the second person can do is listen. When finished, have the second individual retell the story to the group. Emphasize again that the story should have a beginning, a middle, and an end. Do this now.

Step 9: Thank each person as he or she finishes. Have them remain standing there as you ask for the third and final individual to come in. This time explain that the first individual will be telling him or her a story; but as you say this, hand the first person a copy of the story. Tell the new person that he or she is expected to ask questions, have things repeated, paraphrased, and summarized until he or she understands the complete story. When ready, ask the person to please share the story with the entire group.

Step 10: When finished, show appreciation to all three individuals.

Step 11: Review what has just happened.

"The first two situations were examples of passive, one-way communication. What did you observe? Generally, a great deal of remembering has to take place. Often, there is a deterioration of facts, names, dates, times, places, details, etc. Usually it gets worse with each person telling the story. Some portions of the story are often left out or key fragments are held on to and a story (often very different from the original) is built around it. When all you do is listen without reinforcement, it can create serious problems."

"The final telling of the story was the result of active (two-way) communication. The story should have retained much of its basic form with active (two-way) communication. It takes more effort; however, the results are so much better. When people ask for items to be repeated, when they paraphrase, etc., it makes a difference with the results. Make certain that you utilize the tools you have the opportunity to use."

Notes, Insights, and Variations

Unfortunately, even though we usually have the opportunity to use both passive and active communication, many do not permit themselves to use the tools they have access to. Don't allow yourself to get stuck in the passive (one-way) communication rut. A true professional uses both passive and active (two-way) communication for the greatest results.

Story

A woodworker craftsman in northern Montana put a new tin roof on his recently expanded warehouse. That evening, a tremendous storm tore the roof off the warehouse. The next afternoon the roof was located 31/2 miles away. It was twisted and mangled beyond repair. A good friend and lawyer advised him that the scrap tin could be sold to a large automotive company. So the woodworker decided to ship the damaged roof up to the company to see what he could get for it. He crated it up into a very large wooden box and sent it off to Michigan. He marked it plainly so that the automotive company would know where to send the check for the tin.

Fourteen weeks passed without any word from the automotive company. The woodworker was just on the verge of writing to them to inquire further when he received a letter from them. It said, "We don't know what on earth hit your car mister, but give us another 7 weeks, and we'll have it fixed for you."

Say What You Mean— Mean What You Say! 18

Activity Description

TIME GUIDELINE: 15 MINUTES

This fun activity demonstrates the importance of being very clear in our communications to a customer. Is our customer understanding us in the manner we believe?

Learning Objectives

PURPOSE:

This activity demonstrates clarity of understanding. Not only do we need to understand what our customer is saying to us, but, in turn, our customer needs to understand us.

PARTICIPANTS WILL BE ABLE TO:

1. Raise their level of awareness about how they communicate.

2. Recognize the importance of clearly understanding the customer by asking questions.

3. Recognize the importance of using appropriate listening skills.

BENEFITS:

Participants will realize the importance of being understood by their customers as well as understanding them.

Method of Instruction

MATERIALS NEEDED

Sports coat or jacket

PREPARATION AND ROOM SET-UP

An open area large enough for the group to form a circle is required. The presenter stands in the middle of the group.

STEP-BY-STEP WALK-THROUGH OF THE ACTIVITY

Step 1: Have the group form a circle around you. You should wear a sports coat or jacket at this time. Ask for a volunteer or select someone to participate in the activity with you. Have the volunteer stay right where he or she is within the circle. Explain to the entire group that not only is it important for us to understand our customer, but it is absolutely critical that our customer understand us.

Step 2: Focus on your volunteer and say,

"_____ (his or her name), all I want you to do, standing right where you are, is give me verbal directions and tell me how to put on my jacket."

Step 3: As you say this, take off your jacket, and as you are doing so, pull one of the sleeves inside out. Then, take your jacket, placing it in somewhat of a rolled up ball, and drop it on the floor. What follows is often very funny.

Step 4: Be certain that you listen intently and do exactly what he or she says. Have fun with it. If the volunteer says, pick up your coat—pick it up in a ball. Make him or her work for it. Don't assume anything. Should the volunteer tell you to take the jacket by the collar, do so, but with the inside of the jacket facing away from you. If the volunteer says turn it around, do just what he or she has stated. Turn completely around with the jacket in the same position facing the other direction. Or, turn the jacket around and around in your hands until instructed to stop. Don't be too cooperative. Continue with the activity (about 2 minutes) until the usually flustered participant has had enough or accomplishes the task (Some do!).

Step 5: Show appreciation to the volunteer.

Step 6: Ask the group,

"What did we just do here? Sure, we had some fun, but the main point of all this is to say what you mean—mean what you say! Does your customer understand what you are saying to them?"

Step 7: Have participants return to their seats.

Notes, Insights, and Variations

■ Here is some food for thought:

— Pythagorean Theorem = 24 words

— The 10 Commandments = 179 words

— The Gettysburg Address = 286 words

— The Declaration of Independence = 1,300 words

— U.S. Government regulations on the sale of cabbage = 26,911 words
     . . . and that says it all!

Say what you mean, mean what you say.

■ "So, maintain a focus of consciousness that endeavors toward minimization of polysyllabic verbalisms. In other words, keep it simple."   —Robert F. Mager

■ You may wish to substitute the coat activity with the following:

Peanut Butter and Jelly Sandwich
You will need:

■ Jar of jelly

■ Jar of peanut butter

■ Butter knife

■ Loaf of bread in a plastic bag with a tie

■ Table

■ Volunteer

Place the items on the table. When doing so, place the jar of jelly upside down. Everything else is normal.

Say to your volunteer that you would like to have him or her instruct you on how to make a peanut butter and jelly sandwich. You can have the volunteer do this facing you or with any of these other options:

— Back turned to you

— Behind a screen

— Behind a screen with 1 or 2 other volunteers (team effect)

Just as with the coat activity, listen and do exactly what the volunteer says. The results can be hysterical but messy.

Example: If the volunteer says, take out a slice of bread, tear the entire bag open from the middle letting things fall where they may, and then grab one slice of bread very tightly.

When instructed to open the jelly, if the volunteer hasn't noticed that it is upside down, go ahead and open it as is.

Have fun with this one.
The same main point applies: Say what you mean, mean what you say!

Name That Tune! How Moods Influence Customer Communication

19

Activity Description

TIME GUIDELINE: 45 MINUTES

The mood of a customer surely influences us . . . and in turn, the mood we display (consciously or unconsciously) influences our customer. This activity uses sound bytes of music that quickly communicate a mood from which participants describe the type of customer it reminds them of. A discussion takes place around the theme, "Just as our customers come to us with their tune, we are also the music that our customers hear. What tune are you playing?" Strategies are then discussed on types of music to play (moods to create) for key customer events (greetings, dealing with an angry customer, delivering difficult news, etc.), how to play your tune (maintain your mood), and how not to get hooked on theirs.

Learning Objectives

PURPOSE:

This activity will encourage participants to understand the impact of moods in a customer service interaction.

PARTICIPANTS WILL BE ABLE TO:

1. Explain how one's mood influences customer interaction.

2. Describe what mood they usually convey with customers—when that mood is helpful and when it is not.

3. Identify an effective mood for customer interaction and describe how to display it.

4. Describe strategies to create and maintain an effective mood "atmosphere" in difficult situations.

BENEFITS:

Participants will develop an appreciation for the mood they promote during a customer service interaction and learn that the mood often impacts the communication between the customer and the customer service representative.

Method of Instruction

MATERIALS NEEDED

CD player
CDs with four to five pieces of music with different moods

PREPARATION AND ROOM SET-UP

Classroom situation with small groups.

Select four to five pieces of music that communicate distinctly different moods. Moods and examples of tunes include: happy/positive mood (big band), relaxing (folk, easy listening), melancholy (blues), or intense/hard-toned (heavy metal).

Plan to play only about 15 seconds of each song—and discuss how that tune is more influential than the words, if there are words.

A source to download royalty-free music for a nominal fee is freshmusic.com, among others.

Be sure to test the system you will be using to play the music—it is key that it works easily and is loud enough for everyone to hear.

STEP-BY-STEP WALK-THROUGH OF THE ACTIVITY

Step 1: Tell participants you are going to play very short clips of music that represent types of customers they deal with. They are to listen to the music and be ready to describe the type of mood that customer is in.

Step 2: Play a clip of music (fairly loudly), and ask them to describe the mood of that customer—solicit several responses. Move on to the next clip of music, and repeat until all clips are played.

Step 3: Ask the participants how quickly they experienced the mood of the music, which should be "pretty quickly," and how that is similar to interaction with different moods of customers. Conduct a brief discussion.

Step 4: Explain that just as we experience a customer's "music," so too, our customers experience our mood—the music we play within seconds of the interaction. Our mood impacts both the satisfaction and the productivity of the customer interaction.

Step 5: Ask the group to discuss with one or two other people what type of music they think they play in front of customers—their "theme tune." Also, ask them to say when that "tune" works in their favor, and when it gets in their way. (For example: Someone who is perpetually high energy can be very draining to a low-key person.)

Step 6: Ask each participant to write down three important customer connections they have frequently on their job (example: greeting new customers, dealing with dissatisfied customers, problem solving with customers, etc.). Then ask the participants to write down what "tune" (mood) they want to portray during that interaction for the greatest productivity/satisfaction with the customer, and SPECIFICALLY what they could say and do to portray that mood. Have them share their answers with one or two other people and then ask for a few examples from the whole group to share aloud.

Step 7: Ask the group to brainstorm common, difficult customer situations and write them down on a flip chart. Take a quick vote on which ones are most common among the group. Select the top three and for each one ask:

- What type of mood do we need to display in this situation?

- How can we communicate that mood (behaviors—what can we say or do)?

- What can derail us from this and draw us into negative behavior?

- How can we stay "on tune"?

Step 8: Repeat for the other two top priority situations.

Step 9: Ask the group to turn to one or two other people and share what one or two things they will specifically apply to their jobs as a result of what they just learned.

Customer Treatment (Internal and External)

There's an old saying, "If it isn't happening internally, it probably won't happen externally." We must remember that the true definition of customer does not only include the external customer, who must become the very center of our organization, but also the internal customer.

People who work for the same organization must realize that they truly are customers unto each other. Everyday in the work place there are those associates or coworkers who have an impact on us either directly or indirectly and on our ability to be the best professional we can possibly be. In turn, everyday in the work place there are those we influence either directly or indirectly, impacting their ability to be the best professionals they can be. Our treatment and support of each other is critical to our success. These activities will demonstrate that importance for both the internal and the external customer.

The Grab Bag 20

<hr>

Activity Description

TIME GUIDELINE: 15 MINUTES (EACH TIME)

This activity gets everyone focused and back on track, whether returning from a break or lunch or simply reenergizing a group during a session.

Learning Objectives

PURPOSE:

The grab bag activity perks people up, keeps them on their toes, and often brings out some very interesting and creative ideas.

PARTICIPANTS WILL BE ABLE TO:

1. Raise the level of awareness and focus on customer service issues.

2. Promote sharing of ideas and group participation to resolve a problem or question.

3. Challenge individuals to respond creatively to customer service situations.

BENEFITS:

This activity gets people involved and refocused quickly.

Method of Instruction

MATERIALS NEEDED

A bag approximately 6 × 12 inches (preferably cloth—available at the Container Store)
Sets of cards approximately 2 × 3.5 inches (laminated for reuse)
On each set of the cards is a customer service problem, situation, or question pertinent to
the program you are presenting

Note: The card preparation takes a little thought and effort, but the results can be powerful. Here are a few examples of what we have had on our grab bag cards in the past:

- Customer calls and says, "I don't know to whom I spoke."

- Do we treat customers as interruptions?

- The customer has received a defective item or an incomplete shipment. What do
  you do about this?

- You receive a very large order from a customer who is "past due." How do you
  deal with this situation?

- The customer says, "They put delivery charges on this invoice, and I am not
  supposed to be charged for freight!"

- What is the difference between reacting and responding to our customer's needs?

- Why does the customer need to be the center of our organization?

PREPARATION AND ROOM SET-UP

No additional preparation is required. The activity is applicable to whatever room set-up
the presenter has selected.

STEP-BY-STEP WALK-THROUGH OF THE ACTIVITY

Step 1: At any time during a program, you make the statement, "It's time for the Grab Bag!"

Step 2: Have an individual give you a number between 1 and 20.

Step 3: Quickly count off to that number as you move about the group. When you come to the individual the selected number corresponds to, stop and have him or her reach into the grab bag.

Step 4: Ask the participant to select one card and read it aloud. After he or she reads it, ask the participant how he or she would deal with, explain, treat, etc., the situation just described. When he or she is finished, ask the group if anyone has other ideas to offer.

Step 5: Repeat the grab bag one or two more times. Show some appreciation for those who were chosen to respond and then move on with your program.

Notes, Insights, and Variations:

■ After selecting the first participant for the grab bag, let that person have the bag and choose the next responder.

■ Have two or more grab bags and make it into a team competition with scores and prizes for the winner.

When You Were a Customer 21

Activity Description

TIME GUIDELINE: 20 MINUTES

This activity puts us in the shoes of the customer by reminding us of our feelings when we are treated poorly and when we are treated professionally.

Learning Objectives

PURPOSE:

The purpose of this activity is to ask the participants to identify how we should and should not make our customers feel when they are conducting business with us.

PARTICIPANTS WILL BE ABLE TO:

1. Identify moments when as a customer you were not treated as you felt you should have been.

2. Identify moments when you as a customer were treated as you felt you should be.

3. Recognize the impact of professional treatment on your customers.

BENEFITS:

The benefit of this activity is the identification of *how to* and *how not to* make our customers feel regarding the service we are providing.

Method of Instruction

MATERIALS NEEDED

Handout 21.1: List of Feelings

PREPARATION AND ROOM SET-UP

No additional preparation is required. The activity is applicable to whatever room set-up the presenter has selected.

STEP-BY-STEP WALK-THROUGH OF THE ACTIVITY

Step 1: Divide participants into teams of four to six individuals. Select a team leader for each team. Half of the teams are to deal with the following statement and generate a list of ideas and feelings related to the situation.

Situation #1: When you have been a customer yourself, how did you feel and act when you were not treated the way you believe you should have been treated?

The other half of the teams should each tackle the following:

Situation #2: When you were a customer yourself, how did you feel and act when you were treated as well as or better than you felt you needed to be treated?

Step 2: Each team should take approximately 5 minutes to share ideas and develop a list of feelings. When the time is up, start with the more negative comments first—the teams that were not treated as they felt they should have been. Have them share their answers.

Step 3: Now, have the teams share the positive comments they came up with when they were treated the way they felt they should have been and respond.

Step 4: Acknowledge and show appreciation for each team as they finish sharing.

Step 5: A list of responses we have received from others is included as Handout 21.1. The blinding flash of the obvious that needs to be pointed out here is simple: We want our customers to reflect the positive feelings and not the negatives.

Notes, Insights, and Variations

■ Ask if anyone has time to share an anecdote of when they were a customer themselves and were not treated very well. You will find that, unfortunately, many people do have such stories. Ask if he or she would please share the story with the group. When he or she is finished, ask the participant, "How did that make you feel?"

Remember, satisfied customers tend to tell zero to five people about the good service they receive. Dissatisfied customers tend to share the negative service they received with five to ten others.

List of Feelings

Negative

- Uncomfortable
- Embarrassed
- Ignored
- Insulted
- Let down
- Helpless
- Frustrated
- Disgruntled
- Angry
- Cheated
- Upset
- Disappointed
- Annoyed
- Unimportant
- Inferior
- Violated
- Irate
- Hurt
- Unworthy
- Revengeful
- Irritated
- Betrayed
- Mad
- Rejected
- Intimidated

Positive

- Happy
- Pleased
- Special
- Valued
- Elated
- Fulfilled
- Motivated
- Loyalty
- Encouraged
- Shocked
- Important
- Jovial
- Surprised
- Repeat customer
- Tell friends
- Confident
- Respected
- Cooperative
- Generous
- Wowed
- Valuable
- Rewarded
- Content
- Repeat business
- Jubilant

WACTEO 22

Activity Description

TIME GUIDELINE: 15 MINUTES

This activity is designed as a case study for the trainer to read aloud and then lead a discussion as to how each participant or his/her organization would handle it. The story is true; and in most cases, "we've all been there."

Learning Objectives

PURPOSE:

Internal customer service is as important as external customer service.

PARTICIPANTS WILL BE ABLE TO:

1. Promote interaction among group members to discuss how the customer should have been treated.

2. Identify poor customer service and how it should have been avoided.

BENEFITS:

This activity helps us realize that we are all customers unto each other within our place of work.

Method of Instruction

MATERIALS NEEDED

The story by ET of Bloomington, Illinois

PREPARATION AND ROOM SET-UP

No additional preparation is required. The activity is applicable to whatever room set-up the presenter has selected.

STEP-BY-STEP WALK-THROUGH OF THE ACTIVITY

Step 1: Read the following story by ET of Bloomington, Illinois, aloud—or have one of the participants read the story.

> On December 31, 1996, I contacted our company's human resources department to verify my remaining vacation/discretionary time. I said to the representative who answered the phone, "I'm calling to check to see how much time I have left in 1996 to make sure my records are accurate."
>
> The lady responded in a short tone of voice, "You should have called last week!"
>
> "Well," she said, "the records are now purged." In disbelief, I insisted, "Could you please check your purged files?"
>
> She huffed and responded just a few seconds later with how much time I had left. I guess the records were not "purged" after all!

Step 2: Identify the poor customer service elements in the above story.

Step 3: Discuss how the customer should have been treated.

Step 4: Compare the participants' discussion with the response below.

The Telephone "Doctor"®'s Response

Internal customer service is as important as external customer service. The phrase WACTEO should be engraved in the mission statement of every company:

We **A**re **C**ustomers **T**o **E**ach **O**ther

All departments should be trained to respond to each other the same way as they respond to outside calls. There must be no difference. The attitude of "Oh, it's just one of our employees" is not acceptable.

Do whatever you need to do to be sure your internal calls get treated as effectively and politely as external calls.

The People in Your Office 23

Activity Description

TIME GUIDELINE: 60 MINUTES

This activity allows participants to talk about others within their work environment without really focusing on specific individuals. It focuses on personality, values, attitudes, and the real meaning of synergy.

Learning Objectives

PURPOSE:

The purpose of this activity is to openly discuss individuals with various styles of behavior and suggest strategies to deal with them effectively.

PARTICIPANTS WILL BE ABLE TO:

1. Identify the various personalities within their work environments.

2. Define the term *synergy* and relate its application to their own teams.

3. Determine that the real strength of their organization is the differences they possess.

BENEFITS:

The benefit is the realization that *styles* do exist, and the key to success is to adapt and adjust your style to the person and the environment you are in.

Method of Instruction

MATERIALS NEEDED

Six toy stuffed characters: cartoon characters, Sesame Street, something most people will be familiar with.

A suitcase or large attaché case to hold the dolls or characters.

On the cover of the case you may wish to place the name of the company or department you are presenting this to, so that when you lift the lid, it is facing the group with the name properly displayed.

```
Company's Name
OFFICE
```

PREPARATION AND ROOM SET-UP

A table at the front of the room to place your case on.

No additional preparation is required. The activity is applicable to whatever room set-up the presenter has selected.

STEP-BY-STEP WALK-THROUGH OF THE ACTIVITY

Step 1: Say to the group,

"Think about the various individuals you have within your office, department, or workplace. Each one has his or her own personality, values, and attitudes that he or she brings to the workplace. Each also brings his or her own perception of what is going on within that workplace (the good, the bad, and the ugly). Together, however, they make up your internal work group.

"People like this one:"

Note: As you begin to say this and with the cover of your case facing the group, slowly bring the first doll out where its head can be seen and then show all of it. Name the doll using its proper name so that individuals can relate to it (i.e., Daffy, Yosemite, Burt, Tazmanian Devil, etc.).

Step 2: "1. _____ (Name of doll or character). This is a guy/gal who really enjoys his/her work. He/she is soft-spoken, easygoing, and a great team member. He/she doesn't like things that are too risky or too many changes unless things are explained well and understood. When that happens, and he/she feels that he/she is on steady ground, you couldn't ask for a better associate or co-worker."

Note: Hold the doll or character up at about shoulder height as you are saying this. Then ask, "Does anyone have someone like this in their work environment?" Be patient; someone will be nodding in agreement or raise a hand. When they do, toss the doll or character to them and say, "Tell us about that person." Allow the individual time to share. Ask them, "What can you do to assist them in being the best professional, co-worker, or team member possible?" Thank the individual. Ask the group as a whole if anyone has other comments.

Step 3: "2. _____ (Name of doll or character). This is the guy/gal who loves to talk and socialize. He/she is a really good worker when focused on business and the task at hand. He/she needs direction at times to be aware of treating customers the way they would like to be treated."

Follow the same procedure as after the first doll or character by again tossing it out to the individual indicating it sounds familiar.

Step 4: "3. _____ (Name of doll or character). Then there's that individual who is super organized. He/she seems to know all the facts and has all the answers on just about everything, very picky and very opinionated. He/she comes across as pushy and loud at times. He/she seems to be grumpy a lot. He/she tends to find what's wrong (critical) with everyone and everything rather than what's right. He/she needs to be aware that others have opinions that need to be listened to as well as his/her own."

Again, follow the same procedure as before.

Step 5: "4. _____ (Name of doll or character). A nice guy/gal, but not very organized. He/she has difficulty finding things when they need to be found. With the proper guidance, he/she does a super job and tends to be very well liked by everyone."

Follow the same procedure as before.

Step 6: "5. _____ (Name of doll or character). An individual who seems to be more focused on little projects rather than what really needs to be priority one. This person tends to be a real procrastinator and is easily distracted. However, when focused and heading in the proper direction, he/she does a super job."

Follow the same procedure as before.

Step 7: "6. _____ (Name of doll or character). Then you've got that individual who just wants to help with everything. He/she is a friend to all, enthusiastic with a 'let's get it done; I'm here to help attitude.' When he/she is excluded from a team activity or when his/her opinion is not asked for, it hurts. He/she wants to feel that he/she is a contributing member of the team."

Follow the same procedure as before.

Step 8: "7. _____ (Name of doll or character). This take charge, I'm in control individual gets the job done. However, he/she can dominate and push people too much at times, creating resistance. When aware of other's feelings, this person can be very effective in accomplishing tasks."

Follow the same procedure as before.

Step 9: At this point in time, you have seven of these various dolls being held by participants throughout the room. Tell the group that,

"We could go on and on with this, but you understand the point being made here. You can relate each of these characters to a real individual, one of your internal customers, with each one having their own unique personality—the positives and the negatives, the strengths and the weaknesses."

"When focusing on synergy, which we will discuss further in just a moment, consider what each individual has in common that he/she brings to the workplace. It is *differences*. Each brings unique gifts to the workplace—his/her talent, wisdom, skills. These are the items that must be recognized and capitalized on for the benefit of the entire group."

"This is a perfect time to discuss a word that we have all heard, but many misinterpret. That word is *synergy*."

Step 10: Lead a discussion focusing on the following key points of synergy.

Don't mistake sameness for oneness. Synergy is not making everyone the same or attempting to clone people so that we all fit one particular mold.

Real Synergy: We must value the differences between people. The unique differences, skills, and talents that each one of us possesses are the real values that must be recognized.

The Best Answer: The best answer to our challenges is not "yours," not "mine," but "ours."

Synergy Defined: The sum of the parts is greater than the whole; or, 1 + 1 is greater than 2.

Independence versus Interdependence: We can do more by working together than by being independent. True interdependence creates synergy.

Valuing Differences: This is the essence of synergy. This is what gives an organization strength. It is precisely because of the differences that we are as strong as we are.

It takes a special kind of individual to identify valuable differences, grow and nurture them, and bring them together in a significant interdependent manner.

Notes, Insights, and Variations

- This is a great activity when focusing on different personality styles. It would be appropriate to have the participants identify the style of each character as you describe them.

- In discussing synergy, point out that in customer service this is a critical team concept. No one person has all the answers or can solve all the problems, but collectively they are a force to be reckoned with.

The Internal Customer 24

Activity Description

TIME GUIDELINE: 20 MINUTES

When you talk about customers, it is true that the external customer is critical to the survival of an organization. However, there is another customer, the internal customer, and this activity is all about focusing on the significance of that relationship. Many believe that if good relationships and cohesiveness do not exist internally, you will not be able to deal most effectively and efficiently with your external customers.

Learning Objectives

PURPOSE:

This activity should be presented very early in a customer service program. It really demonstrates the impact we have on each other and that we are truly customers unto each other.

PARTICIPANTS WILL BE ABLE TO:

1. Identify those internal customers they directly or indirectly influence, impacting their ability to be the best professionals they can be.

2. Identify those internal customers who directly or indirectly influence them, impacting their ability to be the best professionals they can be.

BENEFITS:

This activity promotes the realization that how we treat each other internally impacts our dealings externally as well.

Method of Instruction

MATERIALS NEEDED

Handout 24.1: The Internal Customer
Overhead 24.1: Internal Customer Impact
Flip chart, overhead transparency, or computer with PowerPoint capabilities

PREPARATION AND ROOM SET-UP

No additional preparation is required. The activity is applicable to whatever room set-up the presenter has selected.

STEP-BY-STEP WALK-THROUGH OF THE ACTIVITY

Step 1:   On a flip chart, overhead, or PowerPoint presentation, display Overhead 24.1.

Step 2:   Discuss the critical importance of internal relationships and the impact individuals have on each other. In the diagram, the upper display reflects you and the fact that every day in the work place there are those on whom you have a significant impact, thereby affecting their ability to be the best professional they can be. The lower diagram represents those individuals within your organization who either directly or indirectly have an impact on you and your ability to be the best professional you can be. Often, if an organization is not successful with its internal customer relationships, it will have a difficult time having successful external customer relationships. It's that important!

Step 3:   Please take the time right now to respond to the questions on the handout (Handout 24.1). Allow 8 minutes for participants to respond to the questions.

Step 4:   Place participants in triads. Have each person within a triad take turns as they share their responses to each question on Handout 24.1.

Notes, Insights, and Variations

■ Have individuals share experiences they have had where the manner in which they were treated by, helped by, or worked with an internal customer within their organization improved or had a significant positive impact on them.

■ Have individuals share experiences they have had where the manner in which they were treated by, not helped by, or not cooperated with by an internal customer within their organization demoralized or had a significant negative impact on them.

The Internal Customer

1. What do I do for others within my organization? Be specific.

   _____

   _____

2. How do I impact their ability to be the best professionals they can be?

   _____

   _____

3. Who are these people? Be specific. Identify positions.

   _____

   _____

4. What do others within my organization do for me? Be specific.

   _____

   _____

5. How do they impact me either directly or indirectly and my ability to be the best professional I can be?

   _____

   _____

6. Who are these people? Be specific. Identify positions.

   _____

   _____

Internal
Customer Impact

What do I do for others?

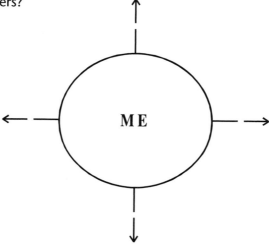

ME

What do others do for me?

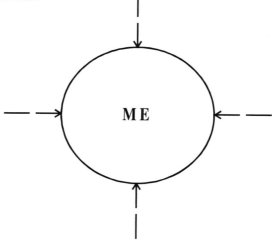

ME

The Golden Rule 25

Activity Description

TIME GUIDELINE: 25 MINUTES

This activity concentrates on the critical importance of treating our customers with the same respect and dignity we would like to receive ourselves. It includes a story, a discussion, and a group project.

Learning Objectives

PURPOSE:

The purpose of this activity is to focus on how we should treat each and every customer.

PARTICIPANTS WILL BE ABLE TO:

1. Demonstrate proper treatment of the customer.

2. Identify specific appropriate behavior with customers.

BENEFITS:

Participants will benefit by the realization that every customer deserves to be treated with the same respect and dignity we would like to receive.

Method of Instruction

MATERIALS NEEDED

Flip chart

PREPARATION AND ROOM SET-UP

No additional preparation is required. The activity is applicable to whatever room set-up the presenter has selected.

STEP-BY-STEP WALK-THROUGH OF THE ACTIVITY

Step 1: Begin by saying, "When speaking about the proper treatment of customers, there is often reference to the golden rule. Not the one that says, 'He who has the gold makes the rules,' but the true golden rule that states, 'Do unto others as you would have them do unto you.' The customer truly must be our top priority and focus."

Step 2: Share the following story with the group:

In Spokane, Washington, a number of years ago a gentleman driving his pickup truck entered the parking lot of his bank, parked his truck, and went in. Now, he was in jeans and wearing a baseball cap, and he looked like a regular customer. He had come to cash a check for $25.00. He made his transaction, got back into his truck, and was on his way to leave the parking lot.

He came up to the exit booth, where a young man said it would cost 60 cents. The man did not want to pay the 60 cents. Money was important to him no matter how big or small the transaction. The young man said he would either have to pay or park his truck, return to the bank, and have his ticket validated by the teller. This irritated the man, but he did park the truck and go back to the bank.

When he entered the bank, there was a line of people waiting for the teller to service them. He waited in line and when he did get up to a teller, she refused to validate his ticket because she did not originally wait on him and was unaware of the transaction he had made. The man said he was not paying the 60 cents for parking and needed the validation. The teller said the only way she could validate his ticket was if he had a transaction with her. He said, okay, I'm about to make another transaction.

It turned out that this individual was a major customer, and he withdrew $1 million and went to a rival bank across the street and deposited it.

Step 3: Tell participants,

"As this story illustrates, we need to treat every customer like they are a millionaire!"

"So many times we've heard similar situations when someone comes into a place of business. They're not dressed that particularly well and usually in somewhat of a hurry. They conduct their business and leave. As the customer exits, one of the customer service representatives comments that the individual is the president, owner, or top executive of a company."

"All the old clichés apply; "Don't judge a book by its cover," "Treat each individual with the same respect and dignity that you would like to receive yourself.""

"What exactly is that treatment that those in the customer service arena should display as professionals with each and every customer encountered?"

Step 4: Divide the group into teams of four to five on a team. Select a team leader. Leaders take their teams through a discussion of excellent customer service.

Step 5: Tell participants,

"Please create a list of behaviors, phrases, and courtesies that reflect proper treatment of customers. Do this now, please." (Allow 6 to 8 minutes.)

Step 6: Have each team present their ideas. List them on a flip chart as each team presents to form a master list.

Notes, Insights, and Variations

Delivering excellent customer service is everyone's job and responsibility. You may wish to share the following as part of your discussion.

A Little Story

This is a story about four people named, respectively, Everybody, Somebody, Anybody, and Nobody. There was an important job to be done, and Everybody was sure that Somebody would do it. Anybody could have done it, but Nobody did. Somebody got angry about that, because it was Everybody's job. Everybody thought Anybody could do it, but Nobody realized that Everybody wouldn't do it. It ended up that Everybody blamed Somebody when Nobody did what Anybody could have done.

—*Anonymous*

A Visit to the Zoo 26

Activity Description

TIME GUIDELINE: 45 MINUTES

This activity promotes team unity and is a great activity to break up more formal studies and reenergize people. This is an activity suited for a larger group.

Learning Objectives

PURPOSE:

This fun activity promotes a lot of teamwork, uses a lot of energy, and has people doing individual work at first to have their team attain success.

PARTICIPANTS WILL BE ABLE TO:

1. Reenergize a group.

2. Promote teamwork.

3. Demonstrate effective communication in accomplishing a goal.

BENEFITS:

The benefit to the participants will be a great deal of fun while promoting team unity.

Method of Instruction

MATERIALS NEEDED

A blindfold for each participant

PREPARATION AND ROOM SET-UP

This activity works best in a large, safe, outdoor area that is blocked off from traffic or a gym-sized room.

15 to 20 participants

6 to 8 individuals to act as safety guards around the perimeter of the outdoor area

Note: This can be done with more participants, but you will require more assistants for safety.

STEP-BY-STEP WALK-THROUGH OF THE ACTIVITY

Step 1: Tell participants to form a line and have one person at a time come up to you as you whisper a zoo animal's name to them. They should not share this with anyone. Also, have an assistant hand them a blindfold. They should not put it on just yet.

As each person comes up, assign them one of the following animals:

- Lion
- Pig
- Dog
- Duck
- Cow
- Elephant
- Cat

Do this in a rotation order so that an equal dispersal of the animals and the teams will be pretty even. If you have an exceptionally large group, add a few more animals. For smaller groups, take away a few. You should have four to six people for each animal assigned.

Step 2: Here's how it goes:

- Participants will gather in a large area, sectioned off and guarded by assistants to protect anyone who wonders off from walking into something.

■ When everyone is inside the area, they will put on their blindfolds.

■ When you say GO, they should begin to make the sound of the animal they have been assigned loud enough for others to hear.

■ The goal is to find all the members of their team who have been assigned the same animal.

■ When they find someone making the same sound, they should join hands with them and continue searching until they believe they have found all their members.

Note: Prior to beginning, you may wish to tell the group how many animals of each kind there are so that they know when the team is complete.

Step 3: When they have all joined up, ask them to form a circle and jump up and down while making their sound to let us know they have been successful.

Step 4: Bring things to a conclusion after most teams have connected. You may lead the stragglers toward their teams to have everyone end up in their proper place.

Step 5: Debrief the group by having an open discussion on how this activity relates to customer service?

Internal customers need to realize the impact they have on each other in getting things done and achieving success.

Notes, Insights, and Variations

This is a terrific activity for a large group. Be extra careful to take safety precautions and have the appropriate number of assistants on the boundaries to protect and offer assistance. It's good for them to shout "you're heading off course" and point participants who are straying in the right direction.

Team Circle— 27
Together We Are One

Activity Description

TIME GUIDELINE: 45 MINUTES

This activity focuses on the unified strength that comes from cooperation and working together. It is a fun activity that is particularly suited for a retreat setting, preferably one outdoors.

Learning Objectives

PURPOSE:

The purpose is to bring all participants together in a fun, unified environment. Participants will be able to:

1. Demonstrate the power of working together.

2. Determine the critical importance of each individual team member.

3. Conclude that "I" may not have the answer, but together "WE" can accomplish the task.

BENEFITS:

The attendees will realize that together they can accomplish a great deal. It is a lot of fun and promotes team cooperation.

Method of Instruction

MATERIALS NEEDED

Microphone

Platform so the instruction can be higher than the group for observation

PREPARATION AND ROOM SET-UP

25 to 300 participants

Setting should be a retreat or grassy area, such as a sports stadium

STEP-BY-STEP WALK-THROUGH OF THE ACTIVITY

Step 1: Have the team members form a large circle—shoulder to shoulder.

Step 2: Say,

"Everyone turn to the right. You should now have your left shoulder to the center of the circle and be facing the back of the person in front of you."

Step 3: Say,

"Everyone in the circle, when I count to 3, I want you all, while still sideways, to take two giant steps toward the center of the circle."

Note: What we are doing is condensing the circle until all the individuals within it form a tight knit group with no spaces.

Step 4: If necessary, have them take another step or two until the circle is tight. Everyone should pretty much have their chin in the back of the person in front of them.

Step 5: Say,

"Now, at the count of 1, 2, 3, sit. I want you (the entire group) to sit down. You'll end up on the lap of the person behind you. 1, 2, 3, SIT!"

Note: This is where things get interesting and funny. If someone isn't listening or is not following instructions or slips off the lap of the person behind them because they are not centered, look out! A portion of the circle will go down similar to a row of dominos. Should this happen, get everyone up and instruct the group how important it is for everyone to cooperate and follow the instructions very specifically. Go back to the first step and start over. Individuals love this, and they want to be successful.

Step 6: When the group is successful at having the entire circle sit down, it is quite a sight. It is usually accompanied by a lot of cheers from the entire group.

Step 7: Say,

"Now, when I say, 1, 2, 3, stand. I want the entire circle to stand back up. Ready? 1, 2, 3, STAND!"

Step 8: Announce,

"We're not done yet. Now, we're going to make this circle walk. Listen carefully. When I say, 1, 2, 3, right, I want everyone to take one large step with your right foot. Then, I'll say, 1, 2, 3, left, and I want the entire circle to take a large step with their left foot. Are you ready? 1, 2, 3, RIGHT! 1, 2, 3, LEFT!"

More cheers! "You did it!"

Step 9: Show some appreciation.

Step 10: Say,

"By working together as a team, you accomplished your goal."

Step 11: Debrief the group by asking participants,

"What did we do? Why did we do it?"

Say,

"As customer service people, you have tremendous challenges. Often those challenges require the efforts of your entire team. That's where our strength is—within the collective energies of the group."

"When everyone cooperated, listened, and followed the instructions exactly, we were able to achieve the goal. When even one individual slipped or didn't follow the instructions, it had an impact on the entire team. It's not a spectator sport!"

"On an individual basis each one of us must give ourselves permission to participate and contribute. Only then can we become fully functional as a team. What an impact this can have on the customer!"

Notes, Insights, and Variations

■ It takes a fully functional independent "I" to be a member of a fully functional interdependent "WE." This is a great statement for discussing how critical it is to give yourself permission to be a member of your team in making the transition from "I" to "WE."

■ You can always have the group take additional steps forward when they are in the circle. If the group wants another task, have them walk backward a few steps.

Essential Tools for Success

What does it take for those with the responsibility to provide excellent customer service to have the means to get the job done? What combination of knowledge, skills, and attitude must exist to obtain the best results? What items must each customer service person have available to them in the work place to fulfill the needs of customers and provide solutions? These activities concentrate on those tools that must be available to succeed. No matter how small or grandiose the tool, if it assists in accomplishing the task of servicing the customer, it is important.

These activities will heighten that awareness of our surroundings, skills, knowledge, and attitude, and how together they impact our ability to achieve excellent customer service.

Check Out Your Work Environment 28

Activity Description

TIME GUIDELINE: 15 MINUTES

This activity will help participants develop an awareness of their surroundings and assist them to be prepared at the start of the day for serving their customers.

Learning Objectives

PURPOSE:

The purpose is to examine the work environment and the tools available to assist in serving the customer.

PARTICIPANTS WILL BE ABLE TO:

1. Determine the tools needed in order to successfully "get the job done."

2. Identify the tools in their work environments that will assist in providing excellent customer service.

3. Recognize that they must be prepared before the first call of the day.

4. Operate by keeping focused on the customer.

5. Show that they are professionals.

BENEFITS:

The benefit will be greater customer satisfaction and more business as a result of being better prepared to deal with and fulfill the customer's needs.

Method of Instruction

MATERIALS NEEDED

Handout 28.1: Check Out Your Work Environment

PREPARATION AND ROOM SET-UP

No additional preparation is required. The activity is applicable to whatever room set-up the presenter has selected.

STEP-BY-STEP WALK-THROUGH OF THE ACTIVITY*

Step 1: Say to the class,

"Did you ever make a call to someone and find they weren't in, and you asked the person who answered, 'May I leave a message?' The person says, 'Sure, but can you wait until I get a pen?'"

Step 2: Explain,

"Your environment has such a great impact on how professional you are with your customers. In order to be as effective and efficient as you possibly can be, it is important to have the right tools in your immediate work environment."

Step 3: Place your participants in teams. Choose a leader for each and say,

"Leaders, please take your teams through a discussion and come up with a list of items in your environment, not only on your desk, but in the office, that would make you as efficient and effective as possible while working with your customer."

Taken from the book EXCUSES, EXCUSES, EXCUSES . . . For Not Delivering Excellent Customer Service—And What Should Happen! by Darryl S. Doane and Rose D. Sloat. HRD Press, 2001.

Step 4: As the teams respond, ask everyone to write down the responses in their notebooks. Say,

"Team 1, please give us three to four items you have come up with."
Ask the other teams to do the same.

Step 5: Share responses by saying,

"Here are some items we have accumulated from other sessions."
Read the list from Handout 28.1.

Step 6: Give out a copy of Handout 28.1. Say,

"When you go back to your office, please take a look at your desk and the office environment and see if there is anything that you can do to improve your tools and how you work with your customers."

Even though some of these items seem simple, they can be very important when it comes to being an efficient and effective professional.

Check Out Your Work Environment

- Computer
- Phone
- Phone headset
- Calculator
- Notebook, forms
- Pen, pencil
- Eraser
- Stapler
- Good technical knowledge
- Humor in the workplace
- List of phone numbers (internal & external)
- Internet access
- Proper computer software
- Clean, efficient work area
- Calendar
- Great attitude
- Phone books

- Good lighting and temperature
- Cover-up fluid
- Facial tissues
- Waste basket
- Fax machine
- Schedule
- Chair/desk
- Responsive departments with answers
- Files
- Catalogs, resource books
- A customer
- Paper clips
- A smile
- Clock
- Self-adhesive notes
- Copier

Learn/Teach/Apply 29

Activity Description

TIME GUIDELINE: 30 MINUTES

This activity awakens the realization that to make training stick, it needs to be shared and applied.

Learning Objectives

PURPOSE:

The purpose of this activity is to demonstrate a basic learning principle.

PARTICIPANTS WILL BE ABLE TO:

1. Demonstrate the concepts to learn, teach, and apply.

2. Identify the steps required to take the knowledge and skills learned in the classroom and make them a part of normal, everyday behavior.

BENEFITS:

The benefit is to assist in the transfer of learning from one individual to another.

Method of Instruction

MATERIALS NEEDED

One potato for every 4 participants
One straw for each individual

PREPARATION AND ROOM SET-UP

No additional preparation is required. The activity is applicable to whatever room set-up the presenter has selected.

STEP-BY-STEP WALK-THROUGH OF THE ACTIVITY

Step 1: To begin this activity, hold up a potato and a straw. Ask the group, "Does anyone think that you can stick this straw through this potato?" Most individuals doubt that this can happen. Call up a volunteer, explaining the following:

"I'm going to teach you how to stick a straw through a potato. You hold the potato in your left hand. Hold it horizontally at approximately waist level. Take the straw into your right hand, gripping it as you would a knife as if to stab something. Now, a critical item to note here is, you must put your thumb over the top of the straw. While holding the potato in your left hand, take two practice strokes with swinging your arm and holding the straw. On your third swing, stab the potato."

"Now, it is very important to swing through, not stopping as soon as the straw makes contact with the potato."

Demonstrate each step as you explain it. Then say,

"Now I would like you to show me that you have learned this by doing it yourself."

Step 2: Coach and assist the participants as they run through the steps. By the way, the straw will actually pass through the potato if these steps are followed.

Step 3: Once they have demonstrated the activity, instruct them to select someone else in the class to teach the skill. Each time someone learns, they move to another person until all participants have gone through the process.

Step 4: Then ask,

"What have we just done? It is a simple, fun exercise with a powerful message. Use it or lose it! If you want training to stick, you have to learn it first; then, teach it to someone else; and then apply it!"

"It's easy to go through a training program, and once finished, set your material down and go back to doing exactly what you did before. The real challenge and the essential tool for success here is to give yourself permission to take the knowledge and skills learned in the training and make it part of your normal, everyday behavior by teaching what you have learned to others and applying it to your real world in the work environment. That's when the training really makes a significant difference, and it truly becomes a tool for success."

Notes, Insights, and Variations

This activity is easy and fun to apply. It fits in easily with your training whenever you want to demonstrate what it takes to make what was learned in the classroom transfer to the work environment.

Unification 30

Activity Description

TIME GUIDELINE: 30–40 MINUTES

This activity pulls together critical components of customer service to achieve a higher level of awareness as to how "everything counts" in building a positive future for any organization.

Learning Objectives

PURPOSE

This activity teaches participants to understand the interdependent relationship of critical components within their companies. Either directly or indirectly, all of the items discussed impact the success of the company and all of the individuals within it. Together, they indicate a time to take action in creating a successful future.

PARTICIPANTS WILL BE ABLE TO:

1. Identify the critical components of customer service.

2. State how each component relates to their company in creating the right future.

BENEFITS

This project often allows individuals to give more value to and understand the significance of the components of their company. They may not have focused on or recognized the value of them in the past.

Method of Instruction

MATERIALS NEEDED

Flip chart
Glue, pins, or tape
16 pieces of paper (approximately 1 × 3 inches)
Container

PREPARATION AND ROOM SET-UP

No additional preparation is required. The activity is applicable to whatever room set-up the presenter has selected.

On individual pieces of paper, write the following or tailor these items to reflect more accurately the components of your company.

- The Right Niche
- The Right Partnership
- The Right Product Knowledge
- The Right Documentation
- The Right Profit
- The Right Order
- The Right Value
- The Right Training

- The Right Investment
- The Right Service
- The Right Fit
- The Right Information
- The Right Responsiveness
- The Right Passion
- The Right Creativity
- The Right Tools

Take the individual pieces of paper, fold them up, and place them in a container for individuals to draw from (we use a magic hat).

STEP-BY-STEP WALK-THROUGH OF THE ACTIVITY

Step 1: Divide participants in groups of three to five individuals, depending on your class size.

Step 2: Go from team to team, having them draw one item from the container each time you come to them.

Step 3: Once all the papers are distributed, select team leaders and have them lead their groups in a discussion of how the item(s) they have selected relate to their company and why it is a critical component of unification in creating the right future. Give each team 8 minutes to discuss the item(s) they selected.

Step 4: On the center of a flip chart, write, "The Right Future." Have each team share its comments on one of the items selected. As the members discuss it, ask others to share their feelings on the topic. When finished, have a group representative come up to the flip chart and glue, pin, or tape the paper to the chart.

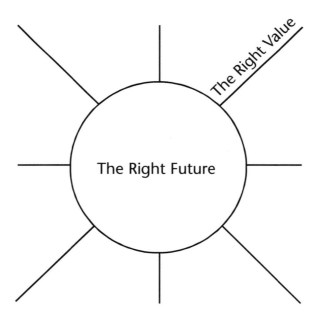

Step 5: This continues with each group reporting, followed by other comments from the group and the placing of the item on the flip chart.

Step 6: When finished, discuss how all of these items together equal the right future for your company. By understanding the significance of each component, it is easier to understand the big picture and how, together, they represent success.

Notes, Insights, and Variations

■ If time permits, you may wish to take this a step further by having participants share which of the identified components they are most impacted by and, in turn, which ones they impact or contribute to.

■ Unification allows people to realize that when all the critical components making up an organization are properly in place, it sets the stage for action. What actions must be taken to create unification for your team, department, or company (be specific) in order to create the right future?

Best Practices in Customer Service 31

Activity Description

TIME GUIDELINE: 40 MINUTES

This activity enables participants to develop their own working definition of "best practices."

Learning Objectives

PURPOSE:

The purpose is to develop a "best practices" list for customer service within the participants' organization.

PARTICIPANTS WILL BE ABLE TO:

1. Identify those practices and behaviors that are essential to performing their roles in customer service.

2. List best practices.

3. Demonstrate best practices through their own performance and behavior in the workplace.

BENEFITS:

The benefit is that the activity serves as a guide for others to follow. It can be applied to new hire orientation, role analysis, or performance appraisals.

Method of Instruction

MATERIALS NEEDED

Handout 31.1: Best Practices in Customer Service
Flip chart

PREPARATION AND ROOM SET-UP

No additional preparation is required. The activity is applicable to whatever room set-up the presenter has selected.

STEP-BY-STEP WALK-THROUGH OF THE ACTIVITY

Step 1: Divide participants into teams of five, and select a leader for each team.

Step 2: Each group is to develop a list of best practices for providing excellent customer service for their position within their organization. They will have 15 minutes to work on this. One member of each team will be responsible for placing their "best practices" on a flip chart and have a responsible person be the spokesperson for their group.

Step 3: Have each group present their findings. Show appreciation as each team completes their presentation. As a total group, arrive at agreed-on best practices in customer service list. See Handout 31.1 for a representative list.

Step 4: Remind participants that this is their list for their company. There is a saying that goes, "People tend to support those things which they themselves create."

Step 5: This is a list they can truly feel ownership of. The challenge is to take this list and implement it into their workplace, making it part of their normal, everyday behavior.

Notes, Insights, and Variations

Best practices lists such as these can become critical components in new-hire orientation, role analysis, performance appraisals, etc. This list may be implemented as a valuable tool within the company. It is particularly powerful because it was created by the people who perform the task.

Best Practices in Customer Service

1. Service, Service, Service with no excuses.

2. Respond to the customer as quickly as possible

   ■ Phone

   ■ Counter

3. Identify yourself, your company, your customer.

4. Educate the customer to the quality of our service and products.

5. Accept responsibility for your own actions and the customer's problems and needs.

6. Always fulfill your customer's commitments and promises. Do what you say you're going to do!

7. Do the work of today—today. Deal in real time in fulfilling your customer's needs.

8. Obtain the correct information.

9. Accept responsibility as a member of a team of professionals dedicated to excellent customer service.

10. Participate in and promote ongoing, continuous improvement.

11. Be a "Master" at what you do.

12. Ask for the order!

Customers and the World Wide Web

Technology cannot be ignored—to do so is to ignore change itself and change equates with survival. As the Internet explodes into our lives, we often find ourselves doing battle for the hearts and minds of Web-surfing customers. The challenge before us is how to capture their attention, give them the proper choices and feelings of control so that we not only capture their imaginations but their trust and desire to purchase and build a responsive relationship.

These activities reflect that challenge to capture the attention of, maintain focus with, and build confidence with each customer that enters our company's domain and to have them leave with the desire to return again.

Think Before Clicking the Send Key 32

Activity Description

TIME GUIDELINE: 35 MINUTES

This activity promotes discussion on the critical significance of e-mail, which has taken the forefront in communications. Much of what we once conveyed to each other in the form of information or facts and figures by telephone or face-to-face is now done by e-mail. As a relatively new vital link in the communication process, it is essential to have a high level of awareness as to the dos and don'ts of e-mail in the business world.

Learning Objectives

PURPOSE:

The purpose of this activity is to get participants to realize the impact of e-mail and the significant role it plays as a communication tool.

PARTICIPANTS WILL BE ABLE TO:

1. Identify the impact of e-mail in the workplace, as well as on personal communication.

2. Identify the pressures and tensions created as the pace of business accelerates.

3. Demonstrate how the wording of a message or the interpretation of contact by the receiver may be misinterpreted with negative consequences.

4. Apply appropriate strategies for the proper interpretation of e-mails.

BENEFITS:

The benefit is that participants will first think about the impact of the e-mail they are about to send and only after a review proceed to send it.

Method of Instruction

MATERIALS NEEDED

Flip chart

PREPARATION AND ROOM SET-UP

No additional preparation is required. The activity is applicable to whatever room set-up the presenter has selected.

STEP-BY-STEP WALK-THROUGH OF THE ACTIVITY

Step 1: This is primarily an open discussion beginning with the following introductory comments.

"E-mails today have taken the forefront in communications. Much of what we once conveyed to each other in the form of information or facts and figures via voice or face-to-face communication is now done via e-mail."

"What impact has this had on the workplace as well as on personal communication? Everything that we send and receive seems to require immediate attention and response. This can often create pressure and tension, and a hurried response may fail to produce the desired results. In fact, often times the opposite may occur when a message is improperly worded or its content misinterpreted by the recipient. And, once the "send" key is pushed, it is on its way, often with copies to multiple recipients who may each put their own "spin" on the way the original message is interpreted. Because we are no longer dealing with face-to-face contacts or verbalization of our messages, our intentions or feelings may not be delivered nor received in the desired context."

Step 2: Share the following story as an example:

"An e-mail was recently received from one of the area managers of a particular company. This area manager had received a call from one of their allied material suppliers. The material supplier indicated that he had spoken with a mutual customer who had recently received service from two of the company's technicians. The message was that although the company's technicians performed the necessary repairs, they did not take the time to perform any update training on the equipment. Our area manager proceeded to inform other managers without first learning more about the actual occurrence from our personnel who had been to the location in question. Word trickled back to the two attending technicians, and they were very upset. When they left the job site, they felt as though they had spent extra time to get the equipment up and running (the cause of the problem was lack of routine maintenance on the equipment) but were really pleased with the job they had done."

"While they were at the customer facility, they met with the company owner as well as the individuals responsible for supervising production and maintenance. They specifically asked these people if there was anyone who needed training on the equipment and were told no. In fact, while they were on the job, the operator responsible for the company's equipment took off to the break area and left the two technicians to fend for themselves. This meant bringing materials to the machine on a tow-motor, performing the routine maintenance procedures ignored by the customer, and staying beyond the allotted job time to make sure everything went right for the customer. It took a considerable amount of time to smooth the ruffled feathers."

"The point to be made is that the original e-mail message from the area manager should have been structured as a question rather than as an accusation. It should have been directed to the technicians themselves and not 'shotgunned' to several other parties."

"Objective: Stop before clicking on the 'send' key. Read your message again and think of the truth and impact it carries. You will be a better communicator for it."

"This is one example of how e-mail was used as the primary tool of communication and resulted in very negative 'internal customer' feelings. Properly utilized, the e-mail could have headed off a potential problem and clarified the situation. Unfortunately, many situations similar to this result as the pace of business and communication increases."

Step 3: Divide the group into teams and select a leader for each team. Instruct each team to spend the next 8 minutes constructing a list of dos and don'ts when it comes to e-mails and their proper structure, content, and usage.

Step 4: Place a sampling of each team's list on a flip chart. Group representatives should then share responses with all participants to create a "master list" of e-mail dos and don'ts. Any other e-mail "horror stories" may be shared (if time allows).

Step 5: Review the master list and conclude that e-mails are now an essential tool and part of the total communication process.

Step 6: Say,

"Properly used, e-mails can be a highly effective tool and enhance communication. However, improperly used and/or abused, not given the proper thought and preparation, it can lead to very damaging results."

Putting Your Company to the Test: 33
Being Your Own Customer

Activity Description

TIME GUIDELINE: 60 MINUTES

This activity has participants playing the role of customers. They will review and critique areas that include internal Web site access, ease of use, and functionality from the customer's point of view regarding their own company's Web site.

Learning Objectives

PURPOSE:

The purpose is to examine the company's web site from the customer's point of view.

PARTICIPANTS WILL BE ABLE TO:

1. Identify company Web site areas that are significant for customers to understand, utilize, and interact with successfully.

2. Use the Web site as a customer themselves to analyze customer perceptions and accessibility.

3. Evaluate the organization's Web site based on ease of use, understanding, order placement, problem solving, and response time.

BENEFITS:

The benefit is that the activity allows participants to experience and analyze their company's Web site from the customer's perspective. This can lead to a variety of adjustments and improvements.

Method of Instruction

MATERIALS NEEDED

Worksheet 33.1: Putting Your Company to the Test: Being Your Own Customer
Computer station for each participant

PREPARATION AND ROOM SET-UP

A shared or individual computer station is required.

STEP-BY-STEP WALK-THROUGH OF THE ACTIVITY

Step 1:   Instruct participants that they are about to put their organization's Web site to the test by playing the role of a customer. Have them take their positions by a PC and instruct them to log on to their company's Web site.

Step 2:   Say,

"Before you begin, I'd like to share an experience with you of our interaction with a particular company at their Web site location with us being the customer. Here are the areas of concern that we focused on."

"While watching a program on television, a product was offered that really caught our eye. We decided to purchase two cans of a natural sugar substitute that was great for the diet program we were on. We immediately called and placed an order. We received the shipment; and after trying it, liked the product so well that we decided to check out the Web site and see if there were any great deals for purchasing the natural sugar substitute in larger quantities. To our delight, there was a discount if it was purchased by the case."

"We logged onto the Web site to place the order and found it was very easy to maneuver. The site gave all the information about the company, where it was located, the various products it offered with discounted quantity breakdowns, and even an e-mail address for customer service. So we made our selection and went through the process of placing the order. It was so easy."

"Within 10 days we received our case of the natural sugar substitute and were very happy with the whole procedure of ordering and receiving it."

"About a week later, the delivery driver came with another package. We wondered what he was bringing because we didn't recall ordering anything else. After opening the package, we found it was another shipment of the sugar substitute. But, we hadn't ordered this. So, back to the Web site we went. Immediately we sent an e-mail to customer service telling them of the mistake. Within an hour we received an answer back saying to return the unopened product to them. But, we had opened it! So we sent another e-mail explaining that it had been opened, and they said they would have to do some checking and get back with us."

"After about 30 minutes, we were contacted again with the message to keep the natural sugar substitute. Were we going to be billed? Another e-mail was sent, and it was verified that we would not be billed because it was the company's mistake. We thanked them with an e-mail. What an experience that was. We were very pleased with the customer service we received and the quick response to our questions in such a pleasant manner. It was almost as though we were talking with them in person."

"What experiences do your customers have when they interact with your organization over your Web site? Is it a special interaction that will have them looking forward to building an even more involved relationship or are they looking to exit and move on, perhaps to the competition?"

Step 3: Assign customer names or codes to each participant for this activity.

Note: This can be used for ease of tracking and identification of the "customer" as part of a learning experience.

Step 4: Hand out and review Worksheet 33.1. Please proceed at this time. When finished, have a general review of the pros and cons.

Notes, Insights, and Variations

Special arrangements must be made for this activity so as not to create any problems or difficulties as this "learning experience" unfolds. When connecting to the site for this training, you may want to have prearranged code names for each participant so that their role playing a customer does not cause confusion for others. Proper preparation is critical for the success of this activity.

Putting Your Company to the Test: Being Your Own Customer

(Circle the response)

1. Ease of use:			
▨ Mobility through the Web site?	Good	Fair	Poor
2. Accessibility to communicate:			
▨ Ask a question?	Good	Fair	Poor
▨ Present a problem?	Good	Fair	Poor
▨ Receive a solution/answer?	Good	Fair	Poor
3. Placing an order?	Good	Fair	Poor
4. Responsiveness?	Good	Fair	Poor
5. Follow-up:			
▨ Tracking?	Good	Fair	Poor
▨ Status report?	Good	Fair	Poor
6. Other:			
▨ Background information on the organization?	Good	Fair	Poor
▨ Who are they?	Good	Fair	Poor
▨ What do they do?	Good	Fair	Poor
▨ Who are their customers?	Good	Fair	Poor
▨ Where are they located?	Good	Fair	Poor

Comments: _____

_____

_____

_____

Part I

Asking for the Order

Nothing happens until somebody sells something—and, we always like to add—*for a profit.* Profit is not a dirty word. How long would a company be in existence if it did not earn a profit? It is absolutely essential that in delivering excellent customer service closure is achieved by asking for the order. All the hard work, experience, knowledge, and skills one uses with a customer is often for naught when we fail to bring it to a decisive, effective, and profitable conclusion.

This section brings the importance of *asking for the order* into perspective. It holds such a vital role in the overall process of customer service, yet it is often ignored, forgotten, or waylaid until all is lost. When you utilize the talents and the gifts you bring to the workplace by professionally working with the customer to build a responsive relationship, fulfilling your customer's needs and delivering solutions, you have earned the right to ask for the order.

Interdependence and Selling Up 34

Activity Description

TIME GUIDELINE: 30 MINUTES

When you are listening to a customer's needs to obtain an order, you also have the opportunity to sell up. This activity focuses on the interdependent relationships that exist between the products and services you provide. Customer service representatives must accept the responsibility that it is up to them to constantly educate the customer about the products and services their organization provides and how these items can fulfill customer needs and provide solutions.

Learning Objectives

PURPOSE:

The purpose of this activity is to emphasize the significance of selling up and knowing what products are interdependently related.

PARTICIPANTS WILL BE ABLE TO:

1. Explain the value of selling up.

2. Identify a variety of products and services and how they are interdependently related.

3. Conclude that it is their responsibility to share information and educate customers.

BENEFITS:

The primary benefit is to advance and enhance the sale. Other benefits include educating the customer about the service and products your organization provides. It also encourages greater product knowledge on the part of the customer service representatives.

Method of Instruction

MATERIALS NEEDED

Paper
Pens

PREPARATION AND ROOM SET-UP

No additional preparation is required. The activity is applicable to whatever room set-up the presenter has selected.
Divide participants into teams of four or five. Select a team leader.

STEP-BY-STEP WALK-THROUGH OF THE ACTIVITY

Step 1: Have each team create a list of five to ten products or services that they will sell or provide for their customers (allow 5 minutes).

Step 2: Tell each team they must identify a minimum of two other products provided by your company.

Step 3: Ask each team to list these items on a flip chart.

Step 4: In a presentation to the entire group demonstrate how those items are related and what benefits/features/positive additions they represent. In other words, sell up! Say,

"Remember, it is our responsibility to constantly educate the customer to the service and products we sell. The customers are not telepathic. The burden is on our shoulders to share this knowledge, reveal information, and provide value."

Step 5: Have each team select two representatives to present their findings to the others.

Notes, Insights, and Variations

As the teams present their findings, gather this information. This can become a very valuable information guide to the products and services a company provides. It may also be a useful guide to demonstrate which items are interdependently related, and customer service representatives can use it to their advantage as they sell up in their interactions with customers.

Achieving Closure 35

Activity Description

TIME GUIDELINE: 40 MINUTES

How do you take all of your hard work, dedication, proper use of exploratory questions, education of the customer, and bring it all to closure by asking for the order? This activity describes four major ways to achieve closure, in order to make all your efforts with the customer worthwhile.

Learning Objectives

PURPOSE:

The purpose of this activity is to bring the selling process to closure.

PARTICIPANTS WILL BE ABLE TO:

1. Explain four major ways to achieve closure and ask for the order.

2. Demonstrate the ability to apply the various closing techniques to actual situations.

BENEFITS:

The benefits are more business and greater profits.

Method of Instruction

MATERIALS NEEDED

Worksheet 35.1: Achieving Closure
Paper
Pens

PREPARATION AND ROOM SET-UP

No additional preparation is required. The activity is applicable to whatever room set-up the presenter has selected.

STEP-BY-STEP WALK-THROUGH OF THE ACTIVITY

Step 1: Have individual participants write down a customer service encounter situation and the method used to close or ask for the order. Use Worksheet 35.1 for this (allow 5 minutes).

Step 2: Review each of the four major types of closure.

A. *The Assumptive Close*

As a result of the dialogue that has taken place between you and your customer, you feel the customer has already made a decision to buy. You simply need to make the move in that direction in order for the customer to indicate his intention.

Example: May I confirm these items with you to be certain everything is correct?

B. *The Choice Close*

The choice close speaks for itself. You are giving the customer two or more items to choose from. This may be a product, service, delivery date, color, or just about anything related to the sale. When the customer makes his selection, you have closed!

Example: Would you prefer for us to furnish the _____ or the _____?

or,

So, which of these have you decided on?

C. *The Yes-Only Response*

This time you're not attempting to create more dialogue. You are looking for a very specific confirmation on the part of the customer that results in closures.

Example: Will this take care of all your needs at this time?

or,

When we deliver this item, shall we make it to your attention?

When the customer responds in the affirmative, you have closed!

D. *Keeping the Door Open*

This close is usually used for those customers having more difficulty in making a final decision. They are riding the fence, so to speak, and require either additional information or a little more assistance to make that final decision. At the very least, you want to keep the door open for a future sale or decision.

Example: What other features or benefits do you require in your decision to make this purchase?

or,

In addition to what we have discussed so far, what else can we do for you to get your order?

Step 3: Ask the volunteers, selected individuals, or each participant (depending on your time schedule) to read the situation they wrote down earlier.

Step 4: As each concludes his or her situation, have the group identify the type of close that was used. Was it the most appropriate close to use having listened to the situation? If not, which of the other closing techniques do you feel would have been more appropriate? Why?

Notes, Insights, and Variations

When the individuals are to share their situations, have them do it in teams. Place participants in teams of four or five. Select a team leader. Team leaders should have each member share his or her story. The team should then identify the type of close used and review the questions below.

- Was it the most appropriate close to use?

- If not, which of the closing techniques do you feel would have been more appropriate? Why?

Achieving Closure

Write out a recent customer situation in which you brought it to closure by asking for the order. Be as specific as possible.

_____

_____

_____

_____

_____

_____

_____

_____

_____

_____

_____

_____

_____

_____

_____

_____

_____

_____

_____

_____

_____

Fulfilling Needs/ Providing Solutions

The days of just providing services for our customers are over. Today our customers want, expect, and demand so much more. We must realize that besides providing services, we are in the business of needs fulfillment. Our customers are looking to us to provide solutions for their problems and concerns.

They want to know how we will impact their organization as a result of the relationship we intend to build with them—their needs, market share, bottom line, and even their future survival. To accomplish this, we must get to know our customers almost as well as they know themselves. Only then can we begin to anticipate change and build a customer-responsive relationship as we fulfill their needs and become a solutions provider for them.

Reacting Versus Responding 36

Activity Description

TIME GUIDELINE: 30 MINUTES

Participants will understand the differences between reacting to a customer's needs and responding to a customer's needs. It involves group discussion and a fun, old-time game.

Learning Objectives

PURPOSE:

The purpose of this activity is to identify key components in building a customer-responsive relationship.

PARTICIPANTS WILL BE ABLE TO:

1. Identify the key components of reacting versus responding to a customer's needs.

2. Recognize the significance of building a long-term customer-responsive relationship.

3. Demonstrate their knowledge of the key components involved with responding to a customer's needs.

BENEFITS:

The benefit is building and focusing on long-term relationships with customers.

Method of Instruction

MATERIALS NEEDED

Potato (one potato per team)

PREPARATION AND ROOM SET-UP

No additional preparation is required. The activity is applicable to whatever room set-up the presenter has selected.
Divide the group into teams of four to six participants.

STEP-BY-STEP WALK-THROUGH OF THE ACTIVITY

Step 1: Tell participants,

> "Remember that old definition of insanity that goes, doing the same thing over and over and over and over and expecting different results? Well, reacting to a customer's needs is much like that. Based on your past actions and ways in which you have dealt with things in the past, you quickly take action, often evaluating the situation after the fact. The goal here is to take care of the immediate problem."

> "Responding to a customer's needs requires much more thought, weighing of the pros and cons, and is based on caring. Your goal here is to build a long-term customer-responsive relationship."

Step 2: Have each team come up with three to five key differences between reacting to a customer's needs versus responding.

Step 3: Allow 5 to 8 minutes for discussion.

Step 4: Instruct each group to share while building a master list. The master list should reflect the following ideas.

Reacting	vs.	**Responding**
Short-term consequences		Long-term consequences
Putting out fires		Building relationships
Quick answers		Right answers
Stressed		Much more relaxed
It just doesn't feel right		The right feelings
Jump right in		Resistance and thought (senses danger)
Ready—Fire—Aim		Ready—Aim—Fire

Step 5: Review and discuss the final list. Emphasize that a true professional actually does both. However, professionals strive to respond to their customer's needs the majority of the time. Reacting upfront can seem quicker and more timely in meeting the customer's needs; but it often results in errors and guessing, which causes rework and doing things over (if you even have that opportunity). Say,

"When you respond to your customer's needs, you are able to do so as a result of getting to know your customer almost as well as or better than they know themselves. This takes time and work, but the results can be powerful in the relationships you are building."

Step 6: Now, for the fun, old-time game. Have the teams form circles (standing). Give each team a large potato. Tell them that they will pass the potato until they hear a loud energetic "stop" from you. You will turn your back to the teams as they are passing the potato around. When you shout "stop," the individual holding the potato is to share what they believe to be an important item to be aware of in building a customer-responsive relationship. The emphasis is on responding to your customer's needs. It's very much like the old time children's game "hot potato." Adults love it, and it provides a great tool for reviewing material. We recommend having them pass the potato three or four times before continuing on with your program.

Notes, Insights, and Variations

■ The potato game review can be used anywhere. It's great fun and makes for an excellent review of material.

■ The concept of responding versus reacting to a customer's needs can be reiterated at various times throughout a customer service training session. It's a great way to keep the focus on the customer. What are they thinking? What are their needs? What impact will what we are doing or discussing have on them? It keeps you customer-focused rather than self-focused.

Transformations and Their Impact: A Reality Check

37

Activity Description

TIME GUIDELINE: 40 MINUTES

Today it is not enough to simply be a provider of services for our customers. We must become solutions providers. In this world of constant change, not only have you experienced many changes as a company, but so have your customers—new changes, new needs, new technologies, and new formulas for success. It will never be the same again; the rules have changed (see Handout 37.1.).

This activity provides an awakening to realities—realities involving ourselves and our customers. The more we are able to know and understand our customers, the more we will be able to anticipate changes and respond to our customer's needs. This activity is a wonderful way to get participants focused on the world of customer service and sales and how it must change with our customers.

Learning Objectives

PURPOSE:

The purpose of this activity is to develop an alertness to change not only in one's own organization, but also in our customers' companies.

PARTICIPANTS WILL BE ABLE TO:

1. Identify transformations they and their customers have experienced in recent years.

2. Recognize the impact these changes have had on their company and its customers.

BENEFITS:

The benefit of the activity is that it builds an awareness that we must be alert to the changes our customers are experiencing in order to fulfill needs, provide solutions, and build customer-responsive relationships.

Method of Instruction

MATERIALS NEEDED

Handout 37.1: Transformations and Their Impact: A Reality Check
Overheads 37.1–37.4: Transformations and Their Impact: Reality Check 1–4

PREPARATION AND ROOM SET-UP

No additional preparation is required. The activity is applicable to whatever room set-up the presenter has selected.
Group participants into teams of four or five, with a leader for each team.

STEP-BY-STEP WALK-THROUGH OF THE ACTIVITY

Step 1:　Select a team leader and then say,

"I'd like to ask you a few questions."

Step 2:　Put up Overhead 37.1.

Ask,

"What transformations/changes has your organization gone through or experienced in the past 5 years?"

Step 3: Tell team leaders,

"I'd like you to take charge and discuss this question with your team members. Write your suggestions down and be prepared to share them. You have 5 minutes." After 5 minutes, say,

"Okay, let's hear from the team leaders."

Step 4: Repeat the question and solicit responses from each team (one idea at a time per team). Write responses on the flip chart.

Step 5: When finished, review the list and put up Overhead 37.2, and ask,

"What transformations/changes have your customers experienced?"

"Keep the same teams, but team leaders should select new spokespersons. You have 5 minutes to discuss this."

After 5 minutes, say,

"Okay, let's hear from the team leaders."

Step 6: Discuss and write responses on the flip chart.

(*Note:* Each of these flip charts should be posted where they can be viewed for comparison and further discussion.)

Step 7: Have participants return to their original seats.

Step 8: Review the changes for both the company and the customer once more.

Step 9: Hand out the paper with the quote on it (Handout 37.1).

Say,

"Not only have you experienced many changes as a company, but so has your customer—new changes, new needs, new technologies, and new formulas for success. It will never be the same again—the rules have changed."

Step 10: Read quote from Handout 37.1:

"If you want to play the game, you must know the rules, and, for the new, improved version of this game, the rules have changed."

Add,

"The world of customer service and sales must change as your customers change—as you change."

Step 11: Tell the participants,

"I have two more questions for you."

Step 12: Put up Overhead 37.3. Read it aloud.

"What do *you* want from your customer? Please discuss this for 5 minutes, and list your comments."

Step 13: After 5 minutes: Discuss and list responses on flip chart. Possible responses: more sales, money, loyalty, more of their customer's time, honesty, openness, etc.

Step 14: Put up Overhead 37.4. Ask the last question to the entire group collectively.

"What will this do for you?"

Step 15: Get responses from the participants and write them on the flip chart.

Possible comments: Stability, peace of mind, expanded sales, profit, money, raises, better life, a future, survival, and so on.

Note: Each of the four previous flip chart pages should be posted where they can be reviewed by the group for comparison and further discussion.

Step 16: Gesture toward all of the flip charts with responses to the four questions.

Say,

"Because all of these realities (which you have noted) really do exist, they create very real needs, the need to anticipate changes and respond to the needs of our customer."

This reality check builds the awareness that in order to fulfill needs, provide solutions, and build a customer-responsive relationship; a keen alertness to the change we and our customers experience must be maintained.

Notes, Insights, and Variations

This can be a powerful activity to lead to further investigation of new strategies and actions required to not only survive but attain the next level of customer service.

■ As a follow-up group activity, have each team develop a list of not only realities, but problems and challenges to be faced as a result of the changes discussed. What do we have to face up to? What problems and challenges must be resolved to make the transition from service to solutions provider? Share results.

Transformations and Their Impact: A Reality Check

"If you want to play the game, you must know the rules. And for the new, improved version of this game, the rules have changed."

—*The New Sales Game**

---

*Darryl S. Doane and Rose D. Sloat, *The New Sales Game*. Amherst, MA: HRD Press, 1999.

Transformations and Their Impact: Reality Check 1

What transformations/changes has your organization gone through or experienced in the past 5 years?

—The New Sales Game*

**Darryl S. Doane and Rose D. Sloat, The New Sales Game. Amberst, MA: HRD Press, 1999.

Transformations and Their Impact: Reality Check 2

What transformations/changes have your customers experienced?

*—The New Sales Game**

---

*Darryl S. Doane and Rose D. Sloat, *The New Sales Game.* Amherst, MA: HRD Press, 1999.

Transformations and Their Impact: Reality Check 3

What do *you* want from your customers?

—The New Sales Game*

*Darryl S. Doane and Rose D. Sloat, *The New Sales Game.* Amberst, MA: HRD Press, 1999.

Transformations and Their Impact: Reality Check 4

What will this do for you?

—The New Sales Game*

*Darryl S. Doane and Rose D. Sloat, The New Sales Game. Amherst, MA: HRD Press, 1999.

Probing the Mind of the Customer 38

Activity Description

TIME GUIDELINE: 40 MINUTES

This activity focuses on the role of exploratory questioning in discovering the real needs of customers through group sharing and the development of proper questioning. The value of creating dialogue is that the customer responds better and we can listen, to truly realize their needs.

Learning Objectives

PURPOSE:

The purpose of this activity is to create dialogue and achieve clarity of understanding through the effective use of exploratory questions.

PARTICIPANTS WILL BE ABLE TO:

1. Analyze a customer service situation to determine how it may have resulted in a better outcome.

2. State the reasons why exploratory questioning is so important.

3. Demonstrate the proper use of exploratory questions to probe for additional information and to have the customer think.

BENEFITS:

The benefits of this activity are to understand the customer's real needs and wants; to help the customer discover, verbalize, and clarify his/her own wants and needs; to let the customer tell you the real issues that are important to him/her; and to know when it is time to advance the sale.

Method of Instruction

MATERIALS NEEDED

Worksheets 38.1–38.3: Probing the Mind of the Customer

PREPARATION AND ROOM SET-UP

No additional preparation is required. The activity is applicable to whatever room set-up the presenter has selected.

STEP-BY-STEP WALK-THROUGH OF THE ACTIVITY

Step 1: Hand out Worksheet 38.1.

Step 2: On this worksheet (working independently) the participants should write out the exact circumstances of a situation they personally encountered with a customer (either over the phone or in person) that for various reasons did not conclude with an order (allow 6 minutes).

Step 3: Place the participants in teams of four or five. Select team leaders for each group.

Step 4: Inform them that the major purpose of this activity is to practice the proper use of exploratory questions. Tell participants,

"Exploratory questions are primarily used to find out people's needs. By asking the appropriate questions, we cause the customer to think more so that they, in turn, talk more and we can listen more."

"Remember jigsaw puzzles? Well, picture a 5,000 piece puzzle and all you have are 17 pieces connected. At best, you can only guess what the finished picture is going to be. Receiving skimpy information from a customer is like that puzzle. We're guessing at what the customer really needs and, unless we change our tactics, may never provide the solutions they are looking for."

"The proper use of exploratory questions allows us to add more pieces of the puzzle until we have clarity of understanding."

"Exploratory questions place the focus on the customer. You are getting them to talk approximately 80 percent of the time while you are only talking about 20 percent. And, when you're listening, you are not thinking so much about what you want to say, but rather what you want to ask so that you can listen more as the customer *helps you* understand their real needs and wants."

"By properly using exploratory questions, you are also helping the customer to discover, verbalize, and clarify their own wants and needs. It's a two-way street as you build a customer-responsive relationship."

"As the customer clarifies their wants and needs, they are revealing the real issues that are important to them. You are now tapping into the customer's perception of reality and no longer just going with what you feel that perception is. Once you fully understand the customer's perception, needs, and wants, you are prepared to take action and fulfill their needs."

"Exploratory questions can be a very powerful tool."

"Here's your assignment:"

Step 5: Explain the assignment and hand out Worksheets 38.2 and 38.3.

"Team leaders: have each individual on your team share the situation they described on Worksheet 38.1 where for various reasons they did not receive the order. As a team, select two of the situations presented and write them down on Worksheet 38.2. For each situation your team is to develop two proper exploratory questions. What do we mean by proper exploratory questions?

■ They must be questions that cause the customer to think.

■ They help to create dialogue, not squelch it.

■ Proper exploratory questions usually start with who, what, why, when, where, or how.

■ It is very difficult to simply answer yes or no to a properly stated exploratory question."

"See the samples on Worksheet 38.3."

"Questions that can simply be answered yes or no can be good questions, but they are not exploratory. We need to prompt the customer to think more so that they talk more, and we, in turn, listen more."

"Remember, the primary purpose of this activity is to practice developing good exploratory questions."

Step 6: Give the teams 12 minutes to work on the activity. Check to see their progress as the time nears and give additional time if required.

Step 7: Have each team share the following:

■ Your first situation

■ Your two exploratory questions

■ Your second situation

■ Your two exploratory questions

The other teams should act as observers/judges to determine if, in fact, the questions are exploratory. If not, correct them together.

Step 8: Show appreciation as each team finishes.

Notes, Insights, and Variations

Depending on the time you have for your program, you may wish to have each team share only one of their final situations and the exploratory questions they developed. However, let them do the entire assignment in their teams. They need the practice. Then, as a team, have them select the one they believe is best to share with the others.

This may be used to emphasize the significance of exploratory questioning and their relationship to fulfilling customer needs.

Say to participants,

> "The responsibility is on your shoulders to constantly educate the customer to the quality of service you provide. Discover your customer's real needs through the use of proper exploratory questioning and sell, not tell! If you're just selling products and services, you're in trouble. You need to be fulfilling needs and providing solutions. Exploratory questioning can help you to accomplish this."

Probing the Mind of the Customer 1

You received a call or were dealing with a customer in person and for various reasons did not end up with an order. Please write down the exact circumstances of your situation below.

_____

_____

_____

_____

_____

_____

_____

_____

_____

_____

_____

_____

_____

_____

_____

_____

_____

_____

_____

_____

Probing the Mind of the Customer 2

Situation A:

_____

_____

_____

_____

Exploratory questions for this situation:

1. _____
2. _____

Situation B:

_____

_____

_____

_____

Exploratory questions for this situation:

1. _____
2. _____

Probing the Mind of the Customer 3

Sample exploratory questions:

- How do you feel about the service we have provided for you in the past?

- How would you explain that further?

- What would you suggest we do in this situation?

- Who would you need to share this information with to make your decision?

- Why is that of such importance to you?

- Where else have you observed that this has occurred for you?

- When might we meet with you to discuss this matter?

Holding On 39

Activity Description

TIME GUIDELINE: 20 MINUTES

This activity focuses on the difference between reacting and responding to our customers' needs and how difficult it can be at times to "let go" of old ways that are no longer getting the job done. We need to replace these old ways with methods that will allow us to fulfill needs and provide appropriate solutions.

Learning Objectives

PURPOSE:

The purpose of this activity is to differentiate between reacting and responding to our customers' needs and to realize that at times we must **let go** of where we are to arrive at where we **need to be** in order to take care of our customers.

PARTICIPANTS WILL BE ABLE TO:

1. State the difference between reacting and responding to our customers' needs.

2. Identify appropriate behavior and actions that allow us to successfully fulfill needs and provide solutions.

3. Conclude that we must build a customer-responsive relationship in order to anticipate change and effectively deal with our customers.

BENEFITS:

The benefit of this demonstration is to realize the role of change in meeting the needs of our customers and in building customer-responsive relationships.

Method of Instruction

MATERIALS NEEDED

Flip chart
Markers

PREPARATION AND ROOM SET-UP

No additional preparation is required. The activity is applicable to whatever room set-up the presenter has selected.

STEP-BY-STEP WALK-THROUGH OF THE ACTIVITY

Step 1: Tell participants,

"Many individuals in customer service feel like they are always putting out fires and are constantly reacting to their customers' problems. In order to build long-term relationships, we must be able to respond to the customer. This means getting to know them almost as well as they know themselves so that we can anticipate change and offer solutions to their concerns."

"I'd like you to listen to the following story."

"Many years ago a lady working as a missionary in Africa had an opportunity to observe how monkeys were captured. An individual would find a large gourd and make a small circular opening in it. He would then proceed to hollow it out. Once finished, he would take this gourd to a location frequented by monkeys and tether the gourd to the ground. Holding up a banana for the many curious monkeys to see, the captor would place the banana in the gourd and simply step away. Eventually, one monkey would let his curiosity get the best of him. There were bananas all over the place, but he wanted *that* one. The monkey could easily fit his hand into the gourd and take it back out again as long as he didn't grab the banana, making a fist. Once the monkey did that, he was trapped. His hand, holding the banana, was his obstacle to freedom."

"*Sometimes people act like that monkey.* They hold onto what they believe is a prize or the way to do something or an attitude, and no matter what other changes are going on around them—no matter what advice others are sharing—they will not let go of that prize for anything. They trap themselves."

"Now, as far as that monkey was concerned, he would try and try in vain to get out of that trap, never realizing that he had imprisoned himself. The captor would simply walk over to the monkey and toss a blanket over him, and he was captured."

"Dr. Leo Buscaglia said, 'Sometimes we need to give ourselves permission to get the hell out of our own way.' How true those words are when it comes to the sales arena. The more you know your customer and your customer's business, the more prepared and willing you will be to alter your method of delivering quality customer service, and to fulfill your customer's needs."

Step 2: Write the words *react* and *respond* on a flip chart.

Step 3: Ask participants: "That monkey was reacting to the immediate problem that presented itself in the only way he knew. What were some of those ways?"

Possible answers: Fear, Panic, Instinct

Step 4: Conclude by saying,

"We have the ability to react, which helps us put out fires, use past experiences, and consider short-term consequences."

"But the critical difference between the monkey and us is that we have the ability to respond to our problems and concerns and those of the customer. However, this ability requires that we think, weigh the pros and cons, know our customers' real needs, and then make a decision."

"Remember the new definition of insanity? Doing the same thing over, and over, and over again, and expecting different results. It's *not* going to happen!"

"You must allow yourself to respond appropriately as we are presented with new challenges from our customers."

Notes, Ideas, and Variations

You may wish to carry the idea of reacting to customers' needs versus responding to customers' needs to the next level. When we react, we focus more on past behaviors, feelings, past experiences, old knowledge and skills, and attitudes. We have more of a tendency to put on what we like to call "the mental straightjacket," saying that's the way we've always done it—I'm not changing for anyone or anything. It's my way or the highway, and if you don't like it, tough! That reactive mindset can result in (and has resulted in) many conflicts and companies that have this mindset simply are no longer in existence.

Tell the participants,

"Responding is based on caring enough to truly focus on that individual who must be the epicenter of your organization—the customer—and getting to know the customer almost as well as they know themselves. When a new challenge comes along, it requires weighing the pros and cons, analyzing the situation, and if necessary, acquiring new knowledge and skills to accomplish the challenge. This all should be done with the appropriate attitude and enthusiasm to move us forward, to accept the demands of customers' changing needs and problems, and to also deal with how these changes impact our own company."

Candid Customer 40

Activity Description

TIME GUIDELINE: 40 MINUTES

This activity focuses on receiving direct feedback from that person who needs to be the center of an organization—the customer. It calls for actual visits to a business and experiencing first hand the service provided.

Learning Objectives

PURPOSE:

The purpose of this activity is to provide direct feedback to an organization from the customer.

PARTICIPANTS WILL BE ABLE TO:

1. Receive direct feedback from customers.

2. Identify the customer's point of view in key areas of concern.

3. Analyze and assess the findings to evaluate current service, performance, behavior, and professionalism.

BENEFITS:

The participants are receiving direct feedback on their service from the most important individual in the organization—the customer. It is a true reality check!

Method of Instruction

MATERIALS NEEDED

Handout 40.1: Candid Customer: The Questionnaire

PREPARATION AND ROOM SET-UP

No additional preparation is required. The activity is applicable to whatever room set-up the presenter has selected.

STEP-BY-STEP WALK-THROUGH OF THE ACTIVITY

Step 1: Tell participants,

"The candid customer activity is a way to receive valuable feedback through the eyes of your customer. It moves an organization away from 'this is how I think we're doing' to the reality of 'this is how we are doing' when it comes to our customer service. If you truly intend to fulfill needs and provide solutions for your customer, then this activity will give you the information required to prepare yourself for that challenge."

Use this as a separate activity apart from a particular session. The results, however, can certainly be shared (and should be) in a variety of customer service programs and even to determine the content of programs.

Step 2: Introduce the concept of the candid customer. The candid customer is a typical customer who has been selected to perform a specific task. That task is to fill out a questionnaire (Handout 40.1) that reflects their perceptions of the company. These comments can become a powerful and useful tool for deciding on future training needs, procedures, and techniques for delivering excellent customer service.

Step 3: Select candid customers. There are a number of ways to accomplish this.

■ A selected team is given the responsibility to interview and enlist a variety of your organization's customers. The candid customer's identity is not known by anyone outside the team.

■ Those having a particular role within an organization such as customer sales and service representatives are asked to provide names of customers they feel would participate in such an activity. Again, a team is selected and given the responsibility of building the candid customer list.

■ Have an outside source conduct such a survey.

Step 4: Once the list is complete (we recommend 10 candid customers minimum per location over a 3-month period with two visits per candid customer each month), put together an information packet or meet with this group to review their responsibilities.

Candid Customer Responsibilities

■ Be a regular customer.

■ Review the response sheet prior to and after each visit.

■ Focus on the six major areas of concentration:

— Environment   — Customer contact

— Expectations   — Responsiveness

— Perception   — Follow-up

■ Record the date of your visit each time.

■ Fill out the questionnaire each time.

■ Be sincere with your comments. We need to hear the *real story.*

■ Turn your responses into the identified candid customer contact.

■ Do not identify yourself as a candid customer to anyone within the organization other than those who enlisted you.

Notes, Insights, and Variations

■ Feel free to use the questionnaire as a guide to construct your own ideas based on your organization.

■ These questionnaires are wonderful "reality shocks" to bring greater awareness to the customer's remarks about a company. A condensed report of the results is a great attention getter at the opening of a session to validate the need for enhancing knowledge and skills in order to meet the customer's needs.

Candid Customer:
The Questionnaire

Six Major Areas of Concentration:

1. Environment

This includes the business establishment, customer service people, management, etc., and the impression you receive when you are there. Is the total environment supportive and encouraging in your decision to do business?

2. Customer Contact

This involves both verbal and nonverbal contact and communication—from an initial greeting (or lack of) to the care displayed through your observed behavior.

3. Expectations

Did they do what they said they were going to do? Did they achieve the level of performance you felt should be demonstrated?

Note: Imagine driving into a full-service gas station and no one coming out to assist you, clean the windshield, etc. You pump your gas, go inside to pay, and the attendant doesn't say a word—not a thank you. Would that be what you had expected? This is what we're after when we refer to expectations.

4. Responsiveness

This involves sincerely responding to the customer's needs and giving the customer's concerns or problems the proper attention by weighing the pros and cons before making a decision and then moving forward with the customer's interest at heart. Responsiveness rests on a foundation of caring.

(continued)

CANDID CUSTOMER: THE QUESTIONNAIRE (CONTINUED)

5. Perception

How does the customer view the business and the treatment they receive? The customer's focus of reality is critical.

6. Follow-up

Will the customer return to do business with this organization again? Is a long-lasting customer-responsive relationship durable as a result of this meeting?

Please respond to the following:

Is the environment you entered one that displays (check all that apply):

_____ Warmth   _____ Cooperation

_____ Friendliness   _____ Order

_____ Caring   _____ Cleanliness

_____ Concern   _____ Peace

_____ Help

Other comments concerning the environment: _____

_____

Did the business meet your expectations?   Yes _____   No _____

Please explain (Did they do what they said they would do?)

_____

_____

_____

How did you feel about the treatment you received and the professionalism displayed?

_____

_____

_____

CANDID CUSTOMER: THE QUESTIONNAIRE (CONTINUED)

Do you feel that your needs were responded to properly?   Yes _____   No _____

Please explain.

_____

_____

_____

Did they take the appropriate amount of time with you?   Yes _____   No _____

Please explain.

_____

_____

_____

Were you asked appropriate questions?   Yes _____   No _____

Please explain.

_____

_____

_____

Did you feel that your concerns were properly focused
on and given the attention they deserve?   Yes _____   No _____

Please explain.

_____

_____

_____

(continued)

CANDID CUSTOMER: THE QUESTIONNAIRE (CONTINUED)

Did you feel rushed?

Were you reacted to rather than responded to?   Yes ____   No ____

Please explain.

_____

_____

Was your perception a favorable one?   Yes ____   No ____

Please explain.

_____

_____

As the customer, did you feel (circle the appropriate response):

Cared about?	Yes	No
Focused on?	Yes	No
A desire to take care of your needs?	Yes	No
Did they make your life easier?	Yes	No
Did they fulfill your needs?	Yes	No
Did they provide solutions?	Yes	No

Will you return as a customer to this business?   Yes ____   No ____

Please explain.

_____

_____

_____

What will you share with others about your visit? Positive/Negative/Other?

Please explain.

_____

_____

_____

Customers' Perceptions: How Their Expectations Are Created

41

***

Activity Description

TIME GUIDELINE: 40 MINUTES

The expectations customers have about your company influence their perceptions of the service they receive. Your organization plays a key role in influencing and creating customer expectations. Customers are "taught" to expect certain things from different organizations by the communications the organizations send to the customer, for example, "We're number two. We try harder."

Customers form impressions of the organization every time they come into contact with something (or someone) that conveys information about your company.

Learning Objectives

PURPOSE:

This activity is intended to help participants better understand customer expectations and the organization's role in shaping and meeting those expectations.

PARTICIPANTS WILL BE ABLE TO:

1. Recognize what customers expect.

2. Understand why and how those expectations were created.

3. Identify some "moments of truth" that occur as a normal part of your job.

207

BENEFITS:

A benefit of this activity is that it develops a greater awareness of the impact of customer expectations and how they are formed.

Method of Instruction

MATERIALS NEEDED

Handout 41.1: Moments of Truth
Handout 41.2: Understanding Customer Expectations
Blank chart pages
Markers

PREPARATION AND ROOM SET-UP

This activity is designed for a classroom situation with a facilitator and participants broken into small groups.

- Photocopy the handouts at the end of this activity.

- Collect at least seven to eight examples of customer communications for the Customer's Perception Activity. Examples of potential communications that could be selected include a poster containing your company's mission, vision, and values; a printout from the company Web site; a copy of a Sunday newspaper ad; a copy of a warranty envelope; a copy (script) from a radio or television ad, etc. Any communication containing messages received by customers are acceptable for this activity.

STEP-BY-STEP WALK-THROUGH OF THE ACTIVITY

Step 1: Introduce and position activity (allow 5 minutes).

> *Note:* To add another dimension to this activity, you might choose to have one group review and analyze a competitor's ad or another type of communication from a competitor. If you choose this alternative, be sure to debrief the activity by comparing the competitive customer communication to a similar communication from your company.

Tell participants,

"The expectations customers have about your company influence their perceptions of the service they receive."

Step 2: Ask participants to indicate, by a show of hands, if they are familiar with the phrase *moments of truth.*

If several participants raise their hands, ask for several volunteers to share what they think this phrase means.

Step 3: Tell participants,

"Jan Carlzon, then CEO of SAS Airlines, coined the phrase *moments of truth* several years ago."

"The phrase refers to a situation in which a customer comes into contact with any aspect of the company or organization, however remote or brief, and thereby has an opportunity to form an impression."

Step 4: Ask participants to suggest some of your organization's "moments of truth."

Emphasize that the really important moments of truth are the cases in which a customer's perception and expectation meet the reality of the organization. For example, if an organization says they have a "no-questions asked" return policy, what would be a moment of truth for that commitment?

(*Answer:* When the customer tries to return something, they will expect to be able to do so easily and will expect that they can return something regardless of how long they have had it or whether or not it is damaged, has been used, etc.)

Step 5: Refer to the Handout 41.1.

Tell participants that this definition of a "moment of truth" is also contained in their handout and that they may find it helpful to refer to it as they work through this activity.

Emphasize to participants that,

- An organization's messages to its customers create expectations or "promises" regarding the type of experience the customer will have when they interact with the organization.

- A "moment of truth" is the reality or "rubber meets the road" situation when the organization needs to actually deliver on the implicit promise it has made to the customer.

- This activity is intended to help participants better understand the expectations of their company's customers.

Step 6:   Refer to the Handout 41.2.

Tell participants to read the directions for the activity contained on that page.

Step 7:   Divide participants into small groups or have them work in their defined "table" groups.

Step 8:   Distribute one of the selected customer communication documents to each table. Each table should have a different example of a customer communication.

Step 9:   Distribute a blank chart page and markers to each table.

Step 10:   Review the directions for the group activity. Each table group will have 10 minutes to prepare a short (1 to 2 minutes) presentation about the communication they were assigned. To help develop the presentation, they should consider the questions listed in their handout and make sure each of the criteria listed is discussed during their presentation.

Step 11:   After 10 minutes have passed, reassemble the small groups to give their presentations. Ask each group to select a reporter to present the results of their table discussion and the information prepared on their chart page. Limit each presentation to no more than 3 minutes.

Step 12: After each group has given their presentation, debrief the activity. Make the following key points:

- Moments of truth are used by customers to evaluate the service we provide.

- Moments of truth are also moments of opportunity. In these cases, we have the opportunity to positively affect the customer's perception of us, either validating an existing, positive perception or possibly improving on a negative perception.

- A very important first step in service improvement is identifying the moments of truth and making sure someone takes personal responsibility for them.

Step 13: Ask participants if, as a result of this activity, they have any new or different perceptions about customer expectation?

Moments of Truth

"A Moment of Truth is a situation in which a customer comes into contact with any aspect of the company or organization, however remote or brief, and thereby has an opportunity to form an impression."

—*Jan Carlzon*, CEO of SAS Airlines

Understanding Customer Expectations

Directions: Working with the other people at your table, examine and discuss your company's customer communication, then answer the questions listed below.

1. Type of Customer Communication:

What type of customer communication was assigned to you (e.g., is it an advertisement, Web page, warranty statement, copy from a radio or television ad, poster, etc.)?

2. Type of Contact:

When would the customer come into contact with this communication? In the store? When returning an item? When purchasing the item? When reading a newspaper or magazine?

3. Formal Message Given:

What information is being delivered to the customer? What conclusions about the company might the customer draw from this message? Are any promises or commitments implied as a result of this message?

4. Expectation Created:

What expectation or expectations might a customer have after being exposed to this message?

5. Moment(s) of Truth:

What "Moments of Truth" are associated with this expectation or corporate promise? Under what circumstances might the customer's expectation collide with "reality?"

Customer Service Assessments

Assessments provide a comprehensive view of the skills or situations that customer service representatives must face. None of us are perfect beings. We are human beings with both strengths and weaknesses or opportunities for improvement. Once an assessment takes place, a new awareness exists. When responded to and acted on, the awareness can lead to greater effectiveness in the customer service arena.

The assessments identified here are activities to complement and support your customer service learning experiences.

Understanding Our DISC Style 42

Activity Description

TIME GUIDELINE: 30 MINUTES

The four styles identified in the AMA DISC Survey™ are utilized in this activity (see Notes, Insights, and Variations). It is a fun group activity that brings together all the individuals who have been identified with a style descriptive of them.

Learning Objectives

PURPOSE:

The purpose of this activity is to share information reflective of a particular style.

PARTICIPANTS WILL BE ABLE TO:

1. Identify attributes reflective of their style.

2. Provide examples of items that reflect the group's style.

3. Develop an awareness that styles do exist.

BENEFITS:

This fun activity will promote understanding and identification of the four styles. It builds camaraderie and the realization that none of the styles are better or worse than the others.

Method of Instruction

MATERIALS NEEDED

Participants should have already received, taken, and profiled their results of the AMA
    DISC Survey™
Flip chart, overhead or slide with the following information:
    Our vehicle of transportation
    Our color
    Our pet
    Our motto
    Our other (three to five other items)
Be creative! Have fun!

PREPARATION AND ROOM SET-UP

No additional preparation is required. The activity is applicable to whatever room set-up
    the presenter has selected.
This activity is best when utilized near the end of a program that has included the AMA
    DISC Survey™ and the adapting and complementing strategies for dealing with others.

STEP-BY-STEP WALK-THROUGH OF THE ACTIVITY

Step 1: Have each participant go to an identified location representing their DISC
         style.

         D – Directing
          I – Influencing
         S – Supportive
         C – Contemplative

Step 2: Select a team leader by group majority vote. Say, "At the count of three,
         point at the individual you would like to lead your group for this activity—
         one, two, three, point!"

Step 3: Display the flip chart, overhead or slide with the following information:

Our vehicle of transportation

Our color

Our pet

Our motto

Our other (three to five other items)

Step 4: Explain the assignment to the groups, which is to come up with an item reflective of their group's style for each of the areas mentioned on the flip chart, overhead, or slide (Step 3). Pay particular attention to the "Our other" section and come up with three to five other items reflective of your group's style.

Step 5: Allow five to ten minutes for group discussion and work. Participants should place their responses on the flip chart that has been provided for each group.

Step 6: After five minutes have past, check the progress of each group and have them select a group spokesperson (not necessarily their team leader) who will present the group's results to the entire class. (If more time is needed, allow for it and adjust your time accordingly.)

Step 7: Announce a *two-minutes-until-show-time* warning so that everyone is ready to go.

Step 8: Decide on a presentation order for the groups. We recommend the D, I, S, C order or the reverse—C, S, I, D.

Step 9: Have the groups give their presentations. Show appreciation for each group.

Step 10: Initiate a group discussion. Ask, "What did you observe?" "What did you learn?"

Note: Each style is necessary. You have some of each style within you. None of the styles are better or worse than the others.

Notes, Insights, and Variations

The AMA DISC Survey™ includes 80 statements that may be descriptive of how you work on the job. The instrument utilizes easy-to-follow instructions and it takes only about ten minutes to review the statements and select your responses. After scoring your responses you will be able to profile your results against those of others. In interpreting your results, please keep in mind that none of the styles being measured are better or worse than the others. Each style has its strong points as well as possible weaknesses. More importantly, all the styles contribute to (or potentially detract from) the effective functioning of groups or organizations.

The AMA DISC Survey™ has been designed and tested to meet the standards for measurements established by such organizations as the American Psychological Association and the American Educational Research Association. These standards specify that surveys of this type should be normalized, reliable, and valid.

Suggested strategies are given for working with people with different styles by either adapting strategies or complementing strategies.

This information comes from the AMA DISC Survey™ and the AMA DISC Survey™ Debriefing Guide.

For additional information on this powerful tool please contact the American Management Association.

What Do You Do? The Gifts You Bring to the Workplace

43

Activity Description

TIME GUIDELINE: 20 MINUTES

This activity focuses on raising the awareness of what each individual contributes to the workplace. It promotes the value of every member of the organization and the significant role each person plays.

Learning Objectives

PURPOSE:

The purpose of this activity is to recognize the unique gifts, talents, and contributions that each individual brings to the workplace.

PARTICIPANTS WILL BE ABLE TO:

1. List the contributions, gifts, and talents they bring to the workplace.

2. Conclude that every individual within their company, department, or team plays a vital role in the total success of that organization.

BENEFITS:

Participants will form an appreciation for each individual within the organization and for each individual's contribution to overall success.

Method of Instruction

MATERIALS NEEDED

Handout 43.1: What Do You Do? The Gifts You Bring to the Workplace

PREPARATION AND ROOM SET-UP

No additional preparation is required. The activity is applicable to whatever room set-up the presenter has selected.

STEP-BY-STEP WALK-THROUGH OF THE ACTIVITY

Step 1: Read this story aloud to participants, then follow-up with written responses to the questions given later in the activity.

"A number of years ago, we were about to take part in a five-day workshop involving college students and adult participants. As I was walking onto the stage area, there was a young man, perhaps 20 or 21 years old, sitting to my right in a wheelchair. As I approached, I could see that this young man was in poor health as a result of some disabling illness. Walking even closer, the young man looked up at me and with slurred speech said, 'Hi, my name is Steve, what do you do?' I replied by saying hi and introducing myself. I told Steve that I was here to be part of the conference and to speak on a variety of topics. Steve replied by saying, 'Oh, that's great, but I'm Steve,' and he said once more, 'what do you do?'"

"As he finished, another young man came and proceeded to guide his wheelchair out onto the stage. He positioned Steve center stage near a microphone. I stood there amazed as the lights went down in the conference center, a spotlight was shown on Steve, and to musical accompaniment, he proceeded to sing the most beautiful rendition of the *Star Spangled Banner* I have ever heard. When Steve was finished, he was met with thunderous applause and a standing ovation. What a performance."

"As Steve was brought back from the stage, once again he paused near me. I complimented him on his wonderful performance. He looked up and said, 'I'm Steve, and I'm a singer; what do you do?'"

"On a popular news station during the tragic events surrounding September 11, 2001, there was a reporter and his camera crew following a fireman as he came out of the rubble that was the World Trade Center. He proceeded to take off his oxygen tank, his mask, shake the ash and dust from his clothes, open his heavy coat, and simply regain his thoughts and energy. After a brief moment, he buttoned his jacket, raised his tank back into position, and was about to put on his mask when the reporter said, 'You're not going back in there, are you?' The firefighter looked at the reporter and his camera crew and said, 'Of course I am; that's what I do, that's my job.'"

Step 2: Ask: "What do you do?"

"Each one of you has unique skills and gifts that you bring to the workplace—items that not only benefit you but many others around you. Your internal and external customers all benefit from your gifts, your talents, and your skills."

Step 3: Give each participant a copy of Handout 43.1.

Step 4: Give participants time to complete the list (about 5 minutes).

Step 5: Tell the participants,

"Now, I'd like you to focus on your list and select one of the positive items concerning yourself; and as we go around the room, I'd like you to share that positive gift that you bring to your company. Be proud of it, and share it with us."

Step 6: When the participants have finished, ask,

"Who should we give these gifts to?"

Step 7: Have a brief discussion.

One suggestion: The customer (internal and external).

Notes, Insights, and Variations

■ This activity stirs interest in analyzing the roles we play within our organization and our relationship with others.

We encourage you to review the "Understanding our DISC Style" (Part K), which refers to the AMA DISC Survey™.

What Do You Do?
The Gifts You Bring
to the Workplace

Write down five gifts (talents, skills) you bring to the workplace. These are things about you.

1. _____

_____

2. _____

_____

3. _____

_____

4. _____

_____

5. _____

_____

Part L

Uncomfortable Situations

Customer service at times can be very challenging. Irate or angry customers can often put our professionalism to the test. However, it is absolutely critical to get over, under, or around the obstacles presented by uncomfortable situations in order to get to the heart of the real concern and begin to address our customers' problems and fulfill their needs. How does one remain cool, calm, and collected during these trying times, reduce anger, and defuse situations to the point at which one can start to respond to the customer's real concerns? These activities will reflect those uncomfortable situations we all encounter.

Real World Customer Encounters 44

Activity Description

TIME GUIDELINE: 30 MINUTES

This activity takes a little upfront work, but it can be a very powerful and effective learning experience. This is a group role play activity to practice as close to the "real world" of customer encounters as possible.

If you've ever been around a teenager, you know what TDC is—Thinly Disguised Contempt—but adults, unfortunately, also use it. And when the heat gets turned up, we tend to employ it more and more. So, when working with customer service representatives or those in contact with customers, this activity will demonstrate how TDC is perceived by the customer and encourage discussion and suggestions as to how we can avoid it, and in its place deliver excellent service.

Learning Objectives

PURPOSE:

The purpose of this activity is to realistically portray the customer's perception and understanding of how he/she are treated, responded to, and serviced by the customer service representative.

PARTICIPANTS WILL BE ABLE TO:

1. Demonstrate the impact of TDC on customers.

2. Role play situations where TDC may surface and how to deal with it professionally.

3. Realize how critical the customer's perception of reality is.

BENEFITS:

Participants will realize how they truly treat customers and that what they deliver should always be perceived as excellent customer service.

Method of Instruction

MATERIALS NEEDED

Script ideas prepared in advance

PREPARATION AND ROOM SET-UP

No additional preparation is required. The activity is applicable to whatever room set-up the presenter has selected.

This activity is done as a series of role plays. The preparation for this is to develop your script ideas that are specific to the group's identity and their particular company.

Scripts should include the following:

- A "normal customer"

- An "upset customer"

- An "irate customer"

- A customer in a hurry

- A customer who wants to socialize

These scenarios should have a basic description of:

- What's happened? "My TV doesn't work. . . ."

- Talking points—it lasted three days, then the remote broke, then the sound went . . .

- What they are seeking—refund, replacement, assistance, etc.?

The scenarios should be specific to the identity of the group.

In each role play exercise, one customer talks to one representative. Depending on the group size, try to have each person be the customer service representative contact person. Others in the group will take turns as customers. For large groups, place participants in teams of four or six members. Select a team leader.

STEP-BY-STEP WALK-THROUGH OF THE ACTIVITY

Step 1: Instruct each team to develop and practice their role play. Two members of the team are selected for the actual role play with other team members assisting with script ideas. When the two team members come up to do the role play, the other team members and other groups become the "observers."

Step 2: Have the observers use a critique chart. They must be on the look out for the representative's use of a sentence that:

    _____ Is accusing

    _____ Is blaming

    _____ Is fault finding

    _____ Demonstrates negative nonverbal communication, and so on

You may wish to add others depending on your knowledge of the group.

Tell the observers to mark their critique sheets each time they observe an occurrence of the items on the list.

Also, look for sentences that could be modified by "idiot." Here's an example: "What do you expect us to do?" Modification: "What do you expect us to do, idiot?" Of course, the way it is said and how it sounds is what is important. If you can add "idiot" to the end of the sentence, if you hear it, you can be certain the customer hears it, too!

The critique sheets are not intended to say, "Aha, you received 20 marks and three accusing sentences. The intention is to point out how often we don't realize the stress in our voice, the attitude we demonstrate, and the caring or lack of it coming across to the customer."

Step 3: Ask the observers, "What should have happened to deal with the customer in a professional manner?" Turn this into a positive learning experience. We've seen the ugliness of negative behavior; now, let's discuss the positive side of excellent customer service.

Step 4: Keep rotating in groups of two until all team members have participated.

Notes, Insights, Variations

■ You may wish to share the following story as an introduction to the role plays. It demonstrates TDC (thinly disguised contempt) and its impact on the customer.

Sam and his business partner, Rebecca, were in the vicinity of a local cellular phone store when Sam asked Rebecca if she would mind stopping there for a moment. Sam had recently purchased cell phones for his wife and daughter from that store. These particular cell phones were the kind with which you purchased minutes of usage upfront and there were no other bills to be concerned with. The problem was that their usage time was running out, and Sam's daughter and wife were having difficulty loading additional minutes from the cards Sam had purchased at the same time that he bought the phones.

Upon entering the store Sam and Rebecca noticed the customer service area with two representatives. One of the representatives was with a customer, while the other was sitting there alone, apparently lost in other thoughts. Upon approaching this CSR (Customer Service Representative), an immediate look of "Now what do you want _____ ?" came over her face. After Sam explained the problem, the representative responded with, "Well this is something that you should be able to handle yourself _____ ! You may have already loaded the minutes and forgotten _____ , and in that case, the card is no longer useful _____ ." (The spaces are examples of when the word "idiot" could be inserted in the mind of the customer.)

Sam and Rebecca throughout the rest of the day spoke of the poor customer service they received, including both the verbal and nonverbal demonstrations of the TDC displayed by the CSR.

Possible discussion questions:

1. Could this situation have been dealt with in a better way?

2. Have you ever experienced TDC?

3. Have you ever demonstrated TDC?

4. Why is the customer's perception so important?

■ Depending on the budget, consider employing actors for the *customer* side. This allows the representative groups to concentrate on the exercise. Good actors will be much more into the negative delivery and get better reactions. Remember, the TDC can be on the part of the customer as well, and the CSR needs to deal with that professionally, too.

■ If contact is primarily or solely over the phone, put a barrier between them and utilize pretend phones (can be purchased from Goodwill for about $2.00).

■ Consider using the customer on a real cell phone. The frustration of poor cell service always adds to the mix!

■ If the contact is face-to-face, set up a counter similar to what is used.

■ Certificates with an "Eliminate the Idiots" logo with a red slash (/) symbol on it can also be developed into a poster for future support and to serve as a reminder.

Training Activity for Customer Treatment 45

Activity Description

TIME GUIDELINE: 30 MINUTES

Often during our daily routine, conflicts develop between those we deal with externally and those we deal with internally. As professionals, we must first realize that in order to move forward someone must attempt to resolve the conflict no matter who is at fault. The following exercise may be used to teach people in any area of business that sometimes conflicts develop because the real needs of each party are not understood.

Learning Objectives

PURPOSE:

The purpose of this activity is to promote *out of the box thinking* to understand and meet the needs of those in conflict and to strengthen a relationship rather than allow it to deteriorate.

PARTICIPANTS WILL BE ABLE TO:

1. Think creatively to discuss real needs in a conflict situation.

2. Identify alternative ways to move a conflict situation forward to a positive result.

BENEFITS:

This activity encourages creative thinking and a drive to resolve conflicts successfully.

Method of Instruction

MATERIALS NEEDED

Flip chart

PREPARATION AND ROOM SET-UP

No additional preparation is required. The activity is applicable to whatever room set-up the presenter has selected.

STEP-BY-STEP WALK-THROUGH OF THE ACTIVITY

The trainer can use the language of the business to make it relevant to the audience.

Step 1: Ask the class to decide on a few issues that are frequent causes of conflict. Be sure to think internally as well as externally because often the internal situations are more frequent and can lead to poor external customer treatment.

Step 2: Ask the class to choose one of the issues that cause conflict. Ask members to state the surface problems. Write these on a flip chart.

Step 3: Ask participants to state the real needs of each of the parties in conflict. What is it they really need out of this?

Step 4: Ask participants to think based on the needs. What are the alternative ways these needs can be met?

Step 5: It will often be discovered that there are several ways to meet the needs once the real need or driving force behind the conflict is made clear. This is an example of *out of the box thinking,* and this exercise can be reinforced with puzzles that require *out of the box thinking.* There are many available. Here is one example:

A burglar broke into a home and stole everything of value but two $100 bills lying in plain sight on the kitchen table. Why did he not take them? You most likely will receive many answers, and occasionally someone will get it. The answer: They were the gas and electric bills.

Notes, Insights, and Variations

This exercise has been used many times when discussing internal conflicts in manufacturing settings where there is often conflict between production versus sales; engineering versus marketing; production versus Q.A.; safety versus manufacturing, etc. It is an eye opener which often shows that parties in conflict actually want the same thing.

Losing Control 46

Activity Description

TIME GUIDELINE: 20 MINUTES

As professionals in customer service, we are often confronted with situations and customers that challenge our ability to remain calm and in control. This activity is about recognizing those symptoms, which if left unchecked can cause us to react poorly, even irrationally, toward our customers.

Learning Objectives

PURPOSE:

The purpose of this activity is to identify the impact of anger upon ourselves and our customers and to develop strategies to use when dealing with these uncomfortable situations.

PARTICIPANTS WILL BE ABLE TO:

1. Identify those symptoms that cause us to lose control and act unprofessionally.

2. Demonstrate professional behaviors and actions to take when a trying situation presents itself.

BENEFITS:

Participants will learn to identify and control their symptoms of anger, which surface when dealing with uncomfortable situations. Participants will also realize that by responding to uncomfortable situations rather than reacting to them there is a greater opportunity for defusing the situation.

Method of Instruction

MATERIALS NEEDED

Paper for recording ideas

PREPARATION AND ROOM SET-UP

No additional preparation is required. The activity is applicable to whatever room set-up the presenter has selected.

STEP-BY-STEP WALK-THROUGH OF THE ACTIVITY

Step 1:   Share the following story,

"A young woman has just had one of the worst days of her life. She had a terrible argument with her husband that started late the night before. After a poor night's sleep, the argument continued that morning until he stomped out of the house, slamming the door. She then called her best girlfriend seeking some comfort, only to also find that conversation ending in an argument."

"Then, while cleaning the house, she knocked over and broke an irreplaceable family heirloom left to her by her grandmother. All this had happened, and it was only 9:15 in the morning. She was upset to say the least."

"Her six-year-old son proved to be in the wrong place, at the wrong time, with the wrong person. While playing with some toys in the living room, he accidentally bumped a vase that shattered on the coffee table. This was the straw that broke the camel's back. The boy's mother exploded, taking all of her anger out on her young son. 'You go out in the backyard and find a stick and you're going to get a beating,' she exclaimed. Well, of course, the young boy was in tears. He obediently went outside while his mother glared at him. She was so out of control that she didn't know what to do with herself as she waited for her son to return. She had lost it!"

"A few moments later her son walked in, the tears rolling down his cheeks. He had his hands cupped in front of him and said, 'Mommy, I couldn't find a stick; will these do?' His hands were filled with rocks."

"Well, the woman quickly regained her rationality. The anger just flowed away as she realized what was really going on."

Step 2: Tell participants,

"Of course, it does depend on the people involved, the circumstances, and the particular situation at hand to determine the best techniques to be used and the rate at which the anger might be defused. You are the best judge of a particular situation because you are the one involved at that moment."

"Anger and uncomfortable situations can get a grip and grasp on us. As you already know, when you enter into an uncomfortable situation with a customer, it can be very challenging. An upset, angry, irrational customer can be very difficult to deal with. It is critical to be able to stay in control yourself in order to eventually defuse the situation. Unless you can control yourself, you may never get to the rest of the problem and resolve the situation. When a situation of this type presents itself, it is critical to remain in control and professional. By recognizing those symptoms that begin to manifest themselves in us, we can be prepared to head them off at the pass, remain internally calm, and dismiss the situation as something we will remain in control of, rationally and professionally."

"On an individual basis, I'd like you to take about 5 minutes right now and list those symptoms that surface in you when you are in an uncomfortable situation. List as many as you can. Examples may include:

- Raising your voice

- Making a fist

■ Crying

■ Grinding teeth, and so on.

"Please do this now."

Step 3: After 5 minutes, place participants into teams of four or five. Select a team leader for each group and state:

"Team leaders, I'd like you to take your group through a discussion and sharing of these symptoms. As each individual finishes sharing his/her list, I want the group as a whole to develop ideas as to how those symptoms might be controlled. Also, what might happen if those symptoms are left to develop unchecked and uncontrolled?" (Allow 10 minutes for discussion.)

Notes, Insights, and Variations

■ This is a wonderful activity to include when focusing on dealing with challenging customers or anger defusion sessions.

■ Another story you may wish to include along with this activity is the following, entitled "Fence and the Nails:"

"A father has been observing his teenage son and how upset, irrational, and angry he becomes over numerous items. The father knew he had to address the issue one day when he saw his son kick the family dog. He took his son outside by their backyard fence. The father had with him a bag of nails and a hammer. Now, the father recognized that his son was a good young man with many positive qualities; however, he simply was not dealing with uncomfortable situations and his anger very well."

"Here's what he did. He said, 'Son, every time you get uneasy, tense, upset, or angry during the next 2 weeks I want you to come out here and take this hammer and a nail and hammer a nail into the fence. This is where I want you to vent, take out your frustrations, and any negative energies you may feel.

At the end of 2 weeks we'll address this again.' The son said he would do this, and that he, too, wanted to deal better with this situation."

"Two weeks passed by and the father and son discussed the results. The son said, 'Dad, I really focused and worked hard to deal with my anger and uncomfortable situations. I hammered 38 nails into the fence.' The father approved of his son's efforts and said, 'Now, what I want you to do is everytime you control your feelings, control your anger, or deal effectively with an uncomfortable situation, I want you to come out here and with the hammer pull a nail out of the fence. When you have removed all 38 nails, let me know.'"

"About 3½ weeks went by when the son came to his father proudly stating he had just removed the last nail. His father congratulated him and said, 'Let's take a walk outside to the fence.' When they got to the area of the fence where all the nailing and pulling of nails had taken place, they stopped. 'Son I want you to notice and be aware of something. First of all, I'm very proud of you and your efforts these past few weeks to work at dealing with your feelings and being more in control of yourself; you've done a great job and you can see the results and benefits. However, there's something else I want you to be aware of. Anger is not something that has to happen. It is something we allow to happen. It is a choice and often a very challenging one. Notice where you pulled out those nails—there are 38 holes over this section of the fence. They are a lasting reminder of negative feelings, uncontrolled temper, and anger that you allowed to exist. Just like those holes, anger can have a lasting impact. It can leave scars and hurt long after we calm down and make amends. If we can control those feelings, head them off at the pass before they result in pain or negative results, so much hurt can be avoided before it ever occurs. What I want you to work on from now on is not just pulling out nails, but never hammering them in the first place.'"

Most Embarrassing Moment 47

Activity Description

TIME GUIDELINE: 20 MINUTES

This activity is a great one with which to start off a day. It involves participants sharing their most embarrassing moment as a customer service person and what they learned from that experience.

Learning Objectives

PURPOSE:

Participants will realize that it is "normal" to make a mistake or to have an embarrassing moment at times. However, they need to turn it into a positive learning experience.

PARTICIPANTS WILL BE ABLE TO:

1. Learn through the sharing of experiences.

2. Recognize that none of us are perfect and that we each have had moments in customer service where things did not go well.

3. Evaluate and learn from negative situations so as not to repeat them.

BENEFITS:

Participants will realize that we all make mistakes as customer service representatives; but, even from those negative or embarrassing moments they can learn a positive lesson and move forward.

Method of Instruction

MATERIALS NEEDED

Paper
Pen

PREPARATION AND ROOM SET-UP

No additional preparation is required. The activity is applicable to whatever room set-up the presenter has selected.

STEP-BY-STEP WALK-THROUGH OF THE ACTIVITY

Step 1: Share some introductory thoughts with the group,

> "None of us are perfect beings. We are human beings each with our own set of strengths and weaknesses. So what we're about to discuss is 'normal,' something each one of us in the customer service arena has experienced. What I'm talking about is embarrassing moments."

> "Please take 5 minutes right now to think about and write down some thoughts on the most embarrassing moment you have had in customer service. Be prepared to share your moment with us and to tell us what you learned from that situation."

Step 2: When ready, tell the group,

> "As we listen to these events, I'd like you to evaluate, critique, and learn from it. Ask yourself what other actions this person might have taken to avoid or prevent that moment from happening then or in the future."
> Take the example below:

"A customer service person was asked to meet with a top executive of an organization. He wrote the date down and prepared for the 9:00 a.m. meeting. In the interim, he misplaced his calendar book."

"On the day of the appointment, he arrived early at the customer's place of business and went up to the administrative assistant, introduced himself, and mentioned the 9:00 a.m. meeting. He was pleasantly greeted and invited to take a seat in the waiting room. It was 8:45 a.m."

"Fifteen minutes, 20 minutes passed by with nothing happening. The customer service person patiently waited, reviewing his notes as another 20 minutes slipped by. He decided to get up and inquire once more. This time just as he approached the assistant, the executive's door opened. The man he was to meet with was escorting another individual from his office. The customer service person and the executive made eye contact and to the customer service representative's surprise the executive said, 'What are you doing here?' The response, of course, was 'Well, I'm here for our 9:00 a.m. meeting.' The executive looked at him and said very disconcertingly, 'That meeting was yesterday.' This was indeed a most embarrassing moment."

What can we learn from this?

- Double check appointments.

- Do not misplace key items such as appointment books.

- Call to confirm.

- Other?

Step 3: Have participants share experiences.

Notes, Insights, and Variations

Have the participants do the assignment, "My most embarrassing moment in customer service" in advance and bring it to the session. This allows for more classroom time.

Your Customer's Perception of Reality # 48

Activity Description

TIME GUIDELINE: 30 MINUTES

This activity concentrates on the power of perception. Not ours, but the customer's. It utilizes a number of entertaining stories and a brief activity to awaken the participants to realizing what a powerful force perception is.

Learning Objectives

PURPOSE:

The purpose of this activity is to realize that the way people perceive things is often not the same, and it is the customer's perception of reality that really needs to be understood.

PARTICIPANTS WILL BE ABLE TO:

1. Identify the customer's perception as a powerful force that determines how and if they will do business with us.

2. Conclude that it is the customer's perception of reality that is the reality they must focus on.

BENEFITS:

The participants will understand the power and the impact of perception and they will see that perception plays a critical role in determining our customers' needs and becoming a solutions provider.

Method of Instruction

MATERIALS NEEDED

Overhead 48.1: Perception

PREPARATION AND ROOM SET-UP

No additional preparation is required. The activity is applicable to whatever room set-up the presenter has selected.

STEP-BY-STEP WALK-THROUGH OF THE ACTIVITY

Step 1: Share the following story with the participants.

"One night at sea, a ship's captain saw what looked like the lights of another ship heading toward him. He had his signalman blink to the other ship, 'Change your course 10 degrees south.' The reply came back, 'Change your course 10 degrees north.' The ship's captain answered, 'I am a captain. Change your course south.' To which the reply was, 'Well, I am a seaman first class. Change your course north.'

This infuriated the captain, so he signaled back, 'Dammit, I say change your course south. I'm on a battleship!' To which the reply came back, 'And I say change your course north. I'm in a lighthouse.'"

Step 2: Tell participants,

"You see, perception can be a powerful force."

"Have you ever noticed when you're driving on the freeway and someone zooms past you and you think or sometimes yell, 'You maniac!' Or you drive up to someone going a little too slow for your liking, and as you pull closer to them, you think or yell, 'You idiot!' Here comes that car going by you too fast—'You maniac!' There's that driver that causes you to slow down—'You idiot!' You have these perceptions because your speed is the right speed. Again, our perception can be a powerful force."

"Look at the overhead please."

Step 3: Put up Overhead 48.1 and give participants a minute to look at this. Then say,

"Here are some quick, fun examples involving perception and looking at things differently. Let me quickly review each."

Note: This activity can be presented quickly with the facilitator reviewing and explaining the correct response to the entire group or you may wish to take a bit longer and allow the participants the opportunity to figure each one out.

Step 4: Point at each example as you review the challenges:

#1—Connect these dots using only 4 straight lines.
#2—By adding 6 straight lines, make 10.
#3—Take 10 dots, put them in 5 rows with 4 dots in each row.
#4—Fill in the blank with the correct answer.
#5—Fill in the blank with the correct answer.
#6—Fill in the blank with the correct answer.
#7—Fill in the blank with the correct answer.

Step 5: Tell the participants,

"Remember, when your customer visits your organization, their perception of the environment they are in has an impact on *both* of you. It is a major determinant of performance and behavior."

■ If the customer perceives an unfavorable or hostile environment, there is a tendency to seek control.

■ If the customer perceives a favorable or friendly environment, there is a tendency to cooperate.

"Do you build/create a comfortable or uncomfortable situation and environment for your customer to function in?"

Notes, Insights, and Variations

Here is one additional story you may wish to insert as part of this activity. Again, it deals with our perception and the way we interpret things.

"A man is driving down a winding road in his sports car. He sees another car approaching. As it gets closer, he slows down because he sees a woman driving and she has her head out of the window. As the two cars come closer, the man hears the woman yell, 'PIG!' The man quickly responds by yelling, 'COW!'"

"The lady drives on and the man, a bit flustered, continues on his way. As he goes around the very next bend he runs right into a large pig, damaging his car."

"When people yell, will you hear opportunities or threats? When people yell, will you only hear what they are saying or will you listen to what they are saying?"

Perception

Looking at things in a variety of ways:

1.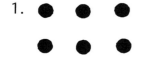

2.

3. 10 Dots
   5 Rows
   4 in a row

4. O T T F F S S E _____

5. J A S O N D J F M A M _____

6. 10 1 19 15 14 4 10 6 13 1 13 _____

7. **1 2 3 4 4 5 6 6 T __**

PERCEPTION (CONTINUED)

(Answers for Overhead 48.1)

Correct Answers:

You may wish to use an overhead marker and show the correct answer on Overhead 48.1 as you review each one.

#1   Most individuals see the boundaries established by the dots. Sometimes we have to go beyond established boundaries.

#2 ||| Add 6 lines to make 10. **TEN**

#3 10 Dots
5 Rows   Make a star and at each place the lines intersect
4 in a Row place a dot.

#4 O T T F F S S E _____
One Two Three Four Five Six Seven Eight
Nine—so an **N** goes in the blank.

#5 J A S O N D J F M A M _____
July August September October November December January February
March April May
June—so a **J** goes in the blank.

#6 This one incorporates #5 in discovering the answer.
J A S O N D J F M A M **J**
10 1 19 15 14 4 10 6 13 1 13 _____
J is the tenth letter in the alphabet.
A is the first and so on.
Therefore **10** is the correct answer to place on the blank.

#7 1 2 3 4 5 6 T ___
This is a mirror image of
1 2 3 4 5 6 7 _____
So, the answer is **8** or **88**

Again, this is just to reflect on the impact of perception and looking at things in a variety of ways.

Customer Service Stories

Real stories—actual experiences that reflect the good, the bad, and the ugly of customer service—can really bring home a message that will have a long-lasting impact on those participating in your program. Relaying these at the appropriate time can reinforce critical concepts, beliefs, and core values.

Service in the News— Do Customers Have to Look the Part? 49

Activity Description

TIME GUIDELINE: 30 MINUTES

Newspaper stories, magazine articles, and television programs constantly provide examples of great—and not so great—customer service. This activity shows managers and supervisors how to make the most of the teaching opportunities. It can be used to create thought-provoking postings at employee gathering places, such as the coffee area or water cooler, photocopy machine, or even in the rest rooms. Or, it can be used to promote discussion during staff meetings or to start off a customer service training session.

Learning Objectives

PURPOSE:

The purpose of this activity is to creatively make the most of teaching opportunities concerning customer service.

PARTICIPANTS WILL BE ABLE TO:

1. Increase awareness of customer service.

2. Provide examples of customer service—good and bad—with tips for providing great service to your customers.

3. Encourage customer service team members to observe customer service in their nonwork interactions and to consider how the quality of that service made them feel.

BENEFITS:

It raises the participants' focus on customer service. It provides a shared learning opportunity of the pros and cons of real life customer service situations.

Method of Instruction

MATERIALS NEEDED

Newspaper articles or customer service stories written in advance along with appropriate thought-provoking questions

PREPARATION AND ROOM SET-UP

No additional preparation is required. The activity is applicable to whatever room set-up the presenter has selected.

STEP-BY-STEP WALK-THROUGH OF THE ACTIVITY

Step 1: Clip an article about customer service or write up the story with proper attribution.

Step 2: Pair the article with your summary of what the story illustrates and how it is relevant to your customer service work. Then, add a thought-provoking question.

For example, you might post:

On February 22nd, WCCO TV's Dimension Consumer Team sent twins Joyce and Joy to shop at major upscale retailers. In almost all cases, the well-dressed twins received faster, more attentive service.

Do you ever judge your customers on first appearances? By tone of voice?

Remember, ALL customers are VIPs and deserve prompt, respectful attention.

Step 3: Post the article, summary, and question at an employee gathering place or use it at meetings or training sessions to begin discussion.

Notes, Insights, and Variations

Want to be sure you have a different SERVICE IN THE NEWS story each week or each staff meeting? Assign each week or staff meeting to a different team member, who will be responsible for finding and commenting on a customer service story.

During a meeting or training session, or on a written comments sheet, ask team members to add their own thoughts about how this story relates to the service they provide to your customers. What lesson can it teach? What principle can it reinforce?

Eureka! 50

Activity Description

TIME GUIDELINE: 30 MINUTES

So much of excellent customer service is based on a strong foundation of caring, confidence, enthusiasm, courage, and attitude. This activity involves a variety of moving stories, each with its own lesson to be discovered and shared by the participants. We call this activity Eureka (Eureka is Greek for I have found it!)

Learning Objectives

PURPOSE:

The purpose of this activity is to discover, discuss, and share the lesson to be learned from each story presented.

PARTICIPANTS WILL BE ABLE TO:

1. Discover the power of storytelling within the arena of human relations.

2. Identify the key lesson within the story and relate it to excellent customer service.

3. Identify the key elements involved in building a customer-responsive relationship.

BENEFITS:

Participants will experience shared discovery and agreement on key issues and values reflecting excellent customer service.

Method of Instruction

MATERIALS NEEDED

Handout 50.1: Story: Remember My Name
Handout 50.2: Story: Always Remember Those Who Serve
Handout 50.3: Story: The Obstacle in Our Path
Handout 50.4: Story: Giving When It Counts
Flip charts

PREPARATION AND ROOM SET-UP

Print appropriate number of Handouts 50.1, 50.2, 50.3, 50.4
No additional preparation is required. The activity is applicable to whatever room set-up the presenter has selected.

STEP-BY-STEP WALK-THROUGH OF THE ACTIVITY

Step 1: Place participants in teams, select team leaders, and distribute a story (Handouts 50.1–50.4) to each group.

Step 2: Instruct each team to read the story out loud and discuss its relevance to excellent customer service. What is the key message or lesson to be taken from the story and shared with the other groups reflecting caring, confidence, enthusiasm, or courage? Allow 8 to 10 minutes for team discussion.

Step 3: Have each team share their particular story and what they have derived from it.

Step 4: Place key ideas on flip charts.

Step 5: Following all group presentations, review the key concepts and ideas, relating them to the critical importance of building a customer-responsive relationship and how it must be built on the foundation of caring, confidence, enthusiasm, courage, and attitude.

You may, of course, add your own stories; however, these handouts provide some powerful ones we have gathered over the years.

Notes, Insights, and Variations

■ These are great stories with many applications. Use them wherever you can reinforce the main idea with a particular story.

■ Share the story yourself with the group to back up and reinforce major issues.

Story: Remember My Name

During my second month of college, our professor gave us a pop quiz. I was a conscientious student and had breezed through the questions, until I read the last one: "What is the first name of the woman who cleans the school?"

Surely this was some kind of joke. I had seen the cleaning woman several times. She was tall, dark-haired, and in her 50s, but how would I know her name? I handed in my paper, leaving the last question blank.

Just before class ended, one student asked if the last question would count toward our quiz grade. "Absolutely," said the professor. "In your careers you will meet many people. All are significant. They deserve your attention and care, even if all you do is smile and say 'hello.'"

I've never forgotten that lesson. I also learned her name was Dorothy.

—*Anonymous*

Story: Always Remember Those Who Serve

In the days when an ice cream sundae cost much less, a 10-year-old boy entered a hotel coffee shop and sat at a table. A waitress put a glass of water in front of him. "How much is an ice cream sundae?" he asked. "Fifty cents," replied the waitress.

The little boy pulled his hand out of his pocket and studied the coins in it. "Well, how much is a plain dish of ice cream?" he inquired. By now more people were waiting for a table and the waitress was growing impatient. "Thirty-five cents," she brusquely replied. The little boy again counted his coins. "I'll have the plain ice cream," he said. The waitress brought the ice cream, put the bill on the table, and walked away. The boy finished the ice cream, paid the cashier, and left. When the waitress came back, she began to cry as she wiped down the table. There, placed neatly beside the empty dish, were two nickels and five pennies.

You see, he couldn't have the sundae because he had to have enough left to leave her a tip.

—Anonymous

Story: The Obstacle in Our Path

In ancient times, a king had a boulder placed on a roadway. Then he hid himself and watched to see if anyone would remove the huge rock. Some of the king's wealthiest merchants and courtiers came by and simply walked around it. Many loudly blamed the king for not keeping the road clear, but none did anything about getting the stone out of the way.

Then a peasant came along carrying a load of vegetables. Upon approaching the boulder, the peasant decided to try to move the stone to the side of the road. After much pushing and straining, he finally succeeded.

After the peasant picked up his load of vegetables, he noticed a purse lying in the road where the boulder had been. The purse contained many gold coins and a note from the king indicating that the gold was for the person who removed the boulder from the roadway. The peasant learned what many of us never understand.

What is that lesson?

—*Anonymous*

Story: Giving When It Counts

Many years ago, when I worked as a volunteer at a hospital, I got to know a little girl named Liz who was suffering from a rare and serious disease. Her only chance of recovery appeared to be a blood transfusion from her 5-year-old brother, who had miraculously survived the same disease and had developed the antibodies needed to combat the illness. The doctor explained the situation to her little brother, and asked the little boy if he would be willing to give his blood to his sister. I saw him hesitate for only a moment before taking a deep breath and saying, "Yes, I'll do it if it will save her."

As the transfusion progressed, he lay in bed next to his sister and smiled, as we all did, seeing the color returning to her cheek. Then his face grew pale and his smile faded. He looked up at the doctor and asked with a trembling voice, "Will I start to die right away?" Being young, the little boy had misunderstood the doctor; he thought he was going to have to give his sister all of his blood in order to save her.

You see, after all, understanding and attitude are everything.

—*Anonymous*

Bonus Section

This section demonstrates the value of humor in the workplace, which, when properly used, can be a powerful bonding force and allows us to laugh in the face of adversity. So much of quality customer service is common sense, that blinding flash of the obvious to treat others as you yourself would appreciate being treated when you are a customer.

The comments collected here lightheartedly reflect those common courtesies and items we should carry with us on our journey of delivering excellent customer service—enjoy!

Being in the Real World—
Collected Bits of "Sage" Advice

Collected bits of "sage" advice along with some new words and their definitions for the work arena:

- The future is not what it used to be.

- Give yourself permission for greatness.

- Blamestorming: Sitting around in a group discussing why a deadline was missed or a project failed and who was responsible.

- Seagull Management: When an individual in a management position flies in, makes a lot of noise, and tends to crap on everything (including those below him/her) and then leaves.

- Be useful, honorable, and compassionate.

- To get something done you need three things: A cup of coffee, a pencil and paper, and someone who has done it before.

- Assmosis: The process by which some people seem to absorb success and advancement by kissing up to the boss rather than working hard.

- Salmon Day: The experience of spending an entire day swimming upstream only to get screwed and die in the end.

- Hurry up and learn patience.

■ Life isn't fair, seek justice, love mercy, and walk humbly . . . anyway!

■ Read broadly, think profoundly, care enormously.

■ Cube Farm: An office filled with cubicles.

■ Prairie Dogging: When someone yells or drops something loudly in a cube farm and people's heads pop up over the walls to see what's going on.

■ No one cares how much you know until they know how much you care.

■ The song you came to sing needs to be sung, by you. Get on with it!

■ Just when you think tomorrow will never come, it's yesterday.

■ Stress Puppy: A person who seems to thrive on being stressed out and whiney.

■ Percussive Maintenance: The fine art of whacking the heck (?-*!) out of an electronic device to get it to work again.

■ Vulcan Nerve Pinch: The taxing hand position required to reach all the appropriate keys for certain commands. For instance, the arm reboot for Mac II computer involves simultaneously pressing the Control Key, the Command Key, the Return Key, and the Power On Key. For Windows it's Ctrl, Alt, Delete simultaneously.

■ When everything else fails, raise your expectations.

■ Imitation is the highest form of flattery. Imitate those you admire.

■ If you mess with something long enough, it will eventually break.

■ Use experience. Your own, plus all the experience of others.

■ Always have something to do, something to hope for, and someone to love.

■ The truly magnificent opportunities only come once. Seize life.

■ Adminisphere: The rarefied organizational layers beginning just above the rank and file. Decisions that fall from the adminisphere are often profoundly inappropriate or irrelevant to the problems they were designed to solve.

■ 404: Someone who's clueless. From the World Wide Web error message "404 Not Found," meaning that the requested document could not be located.

- OHNOSECOND: That minuscule fraction of time in which you realize that you've just made a BIG mistake.

- We all screw up, but in different ways. Forgiveness is essential to survival. We need to forgive others and we must work at forgiving ourselves . . . then forget it and get on with life.

- People tend to support those things that they themselves create.

- Realize that you are unique in the world—you have a magnificent contribution that only you can give. The world needs you desperately.

Appendix A

The Documenter
Learning Tool

The Customer
Service Documenter

There is an old saying that goes, "People tend to support those things that they themselves create." It enhances feelings of ownership and personal pride, and it adds focus of attention, caring, and involvement.

The Documenter represents an ongoing process of continuous improvement through both individual and team disclosures and the sharing of customer service situations. Through the documentation of "special-learning" customer service moments it will allow for discussion, examination, analysis, and identification of both proper and improper behavior and actions with customers. It will help attain an awareness of what should have happened and how this situation will be best dealt with in the future.

The Documenter will assist in the accomplishment of the following:

- The identification of "special-learning" customer service moments for your organization.

- The indication of the appropriate behavior and actions to take for the delivery of excellent customer service.

- The promotion of effective communication and the sharing of customer service interactions between all components of the customer service arena.

- The identification of and the continuous improvement of the level of customer service expectations.

- The ongoing development of a bank of knowledge and skills generated from specific customer service situations.

- The development of action plans for dealing with customer service situations that have been identified and are specific to your organization.

Method of Instruction

- Please refer to the accompanying "Documenter" pages included with this manual. These are intended to provide you with a starter template for your own customer service applications.

- Personal interview and use of after situation review (ASR)

- Documenter information

- Application for:

    ___ Individual use

    ___ Group discussion

- Action Plans:

    ___ Strategies

    ___ Implementation

The Documenter's primary function is the documentation, collection, and gathering of input from your customer service people. It focuses on the identification of "special-learning" moments using the after situation review, or ASR. This then becomes a valuable collection, uniquely representing your organization and its own interactions with customers. It is a powerful tool with many applications:

- Meetings

- New hires

- Role plays

- Refreshers

- Other

AFTER SITUATION REVIEW

The ASR may take place after every customer service situation selected as a "learning experience."

The customer sales and service representative (CSSR) sits down with the appropriate supervisor (CSSR manager, director, etc.) who becomes the observer and they decide whether this situation is to be included as a special learning situation and included in the Documenter.

The process is as follows:

1. Customer service situation occurs.

2. CSSR brings it to the attention of the designated supervisor.

3. They discuss what happened in order to thoroughly understand the situation. This verifies exactly what occurred and when.

4. Questions to be raised by the supervision:

    a. As a learning experience, how could this impact and improve individual performance?

    b. As a learning experience, how could this impact and improve team performance?

    c. What do you believe could have been done to improve the situation?

    d. What do you think your team would have wanted you to do in this situation?

   Raise any other pertinent question to fully understand the significance of the event.

Note: Taking the time to create the necessary dialogue for full understanding and dissection of the customer service situation is critical. Yes, it is an investment of precious time, but the return on performance (and isn't that what we're after?) can be very high.

This type of learning is very powerful once participants get over the uncomfortable feelings of discussing their own performance gaps (which we all have, by the way). Remember, the goal here is not criticism or singling out individuals to pick on. The goal is to create an ongoing process of learning based on real-life situations as related by your own people.

Following a thorough discussion of the situation, a decision is made whether or not to include this event on the Documenter to be among the "special-learning" customer service moments.

This becomes a powerful documentation tool, specifically related to your own company. There are many potential applications.

- New hire orientation

- Inclusion as role plays for meetings

- Individual review and updating of skills

- Comparison to other similar occurrences and the proper handling of a situation

- Allows CSSRs to be more proactive and prepared for similar situations as they surface

DOCUMENTER SET-UP

Title: What would you do?

Documentation of customer service situations:

Section I   Documentation

- Exactly what happened? Describe the service encounter as specifically as possible.

- How did you deal with the situation yourself?

- In review, what else might you have done?

Section II   Input from Others

- How would you have dealt with this situation?

- What would you have done differently?

- What would you not have done that occurred in the original encounter? Be specific—comments that were made; verbal and nonverbal communicators.

Section III   Action Plan

■ When a similar situation takes place, these are items of particular significance that I need:

— to be aware of

— alert to

— be certain to do

— be certain to avoid

Note: The Documenter can become a valuable, unique learning tool for your organization. Facilitators will discover the Documenter to have numerous applications for real world experiences. It provides you with a template to develop your own library of documented customer service activities.

The Documenter

Introductory Comments

The Documenter represents an ongoing process of continuous improvement through both individual and team disclosures and sharing of customer service situations. Through the documentation of "special-learning" customer service moments,* it will allow for discussion, examination, analysis, and identification of both proper and improper behavior and actions with customers. For any negative customer-related situation, awareness will be attained of what should have happened and how the situation will best be dealt with in the future.

The Documenter will assist in the accomplishment of the following:

- Identify "special-learning" customer service moments for your organization.

- Indicate the appropriate behavior and actions necessary to deliver excellent customer service.

- Promote effective communication and sharing of customer service interactions between all components of the customer service arena.

- Identify and continuously improve the level of customer service expectations.

- Continually develop a bank of knowledge and skills generated from specific customer service situations.

- Develop action plans for dealing with customer service situations that have been identified and are specific to your organization.

The primary function of using the Documenter is to document, collect, and gather input from your customer service people. The materials to be documented are those items that have been selected as a result of the identification of "special-learning"

* A "special-learning" customer service moment is an interaction between a customer service representative and a customer either in person, over the telephone, or other means of communication (Internet, Web site, e-mail) that has been recognized as having learning capabilities for others within the organizations.

THE DOCUMENTER (CONTINUED)

moments using the ASR (after situation review). This then becomes a valuable collection uniquely representing your organization and its own interactions with customers. What a powerful tool this can be with so many applications such as:

- Meetings
- New hires
- Role plays
- Refreshers
- Other

CONGRATULATIONS!

Your ASR (after situation review) has determined that the customer service encounter you shared has been selected to become a "learning experience" for your organization.

Note: See ASR in the Documenter Appendix A of your manual.

SECTION I: DOCUMENTATION

- Exactly what happened? Describe the service encounter as specifically as possible.

_____

_____

_____

_____

_____

_____

_____

_____

_____

_____

(continued)

THE DOCUMENTER (CONTINUED)

■ How did you deal with the situation yourself? What actions did you take?

_____

_____

_____

_____

_____

_____

_____

_____

_____

■ In review, what else do you feel you might have done to have a more effective outcome—for your customer, for yourself, for your company?

_____

_____

_____

_____

_____

_____

_____

_____

_____

SECTION II: INPUT FROM OTHERS

This may include individual and/or group input. Your facilitator will instruct you on this.

■ How would you have dealt with this situation?

_____

_____

THE DOCUMENTER (CONTINUED)

_____

_____

_____

_____

_____

_____

_____

■ What do you feel was done properly for the situation described?

_____

_____

_____

_____

_____

_____

_____

■ What do you believe the customer service person should have done differently?

_____

_____

_____

_____

_____

_____

_____

_____

(continued)

THE DOCUMENTER (CONTINUED)

■ What would you not have done that occurred in the original encounter? Be as specific as possible. Include comments that were made, verbal and nonverbal communication, follow-up, and other ideas.

_____

_____

_____

_____

_____

_____

_____

_____

_____

SECTION III: ACTION PLAN

When a similar customer service situation takes place, these are items of particular significance that I need to be:

■ Aware of

_____

_____

_____

_____

_____

■ Alert to

_____

_____

_____

_____

_____

THE DOCUMENTER (CONTINUED)

■ Certain to do

_____

_____

_____

_____

_____

■ Certain to avoid doing

_____

_____

_____

_____

_____

■ Other

_____

_____

_____

_____

_____

Note: Repeat this template for each customer service situation you wish to document and include as part of this resource material.

Appendix B

Customer Service Reminders

The following are taken from our book, *EXCUSES, EXCUSES, EXCUSES . . . For Not Delivering Excellent Customer Service—And What Should Happen!* They may be used in a variety of ways to complement and support your constant quest for excellent customer service:

- Reproduced and used as inspirational posters

- Made into overheads for use during customer service training

- Added to PowerPoint presentations

- Included as sectional dividers for your customer service notebooks/training programs

- Constant reminders of the need to deliver excellent customer service with no excuses

There should be no excuses for not delivering excellent customer service.

If the customer
is not the
central concern
of your
organization,
you may not
have an
organization
to be
concerned
about.

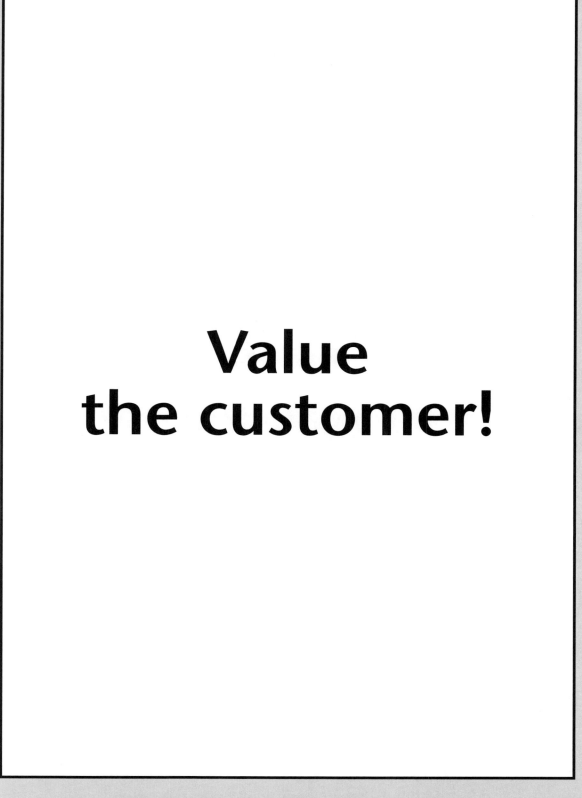

Value
the customer!

Provide on-time service and do it responsibly, responsively, and repeatedly!

The customer must be number one!

Make the customer the center of your organization!

The customer's perception of reality is the reality you must deal with!

You must have a passion for delivering excellent customer service.

Where would you be without your customers?

Your customers expect excellent service!

You are in the needs fulfillment business!

AUTHOR BIOGRAPHIES

Darryl S. Doane and Rose D. Sloat

Darryl S. Doane has served as a teacher, speaker, facilitator, and professional consultant for more than 30 years. He has presented outstanding programs to numerous organizations, including adult, college, and youth organizations, churches, civic groups, and corporate America. He has worked with national organizations, such as the National Association of Student Councils and Secondary Schools Principals, and was a participant in NASA's Teacher in Space Program. He served as Senior Training Specialist for a billion-dollar corporation for seven years before becoming a managing partner and cocreator of The Learning Service, Ltd., with his partner Rose.

Rose D. Sloat served as the training coordinator of a billion-dollar company for 15 years. She is an outstanding facilitator who has learned, taught, and applied every component within the training arena from organizing and scheduling training to writing and producing learning events. Rose has enabled The Learning Service, Ltd., to become an effective and efficient means of quality learning for companies who have chosen to outsource their training needs. She serves on the board of a support group for women (WIN, Women's Initiative) in the capacity of Vice President. She also is currently an officer of a local Toastmasters Club #3342 and holds the position of Vice President of Education. Rose is a managing partner and cocreator of The Learning Service, Ltd.

In addition to *The Customer Service Activity Book*, **Rose D. Sloat** and **Darryl S. Doane** have coauthored *The New Sales Game,* a program focusing on the outside sales force and the quest to move from service to solutions providers and *The New Sales Game Participants Book.* They are also coauthors of the book, *EXCUSES, EXCUSES, EXCUSES . . . For Not Delivering Excellent Customer Service—And What Should Happen!* In addition, they are the coauthors and editors of *50 Activities for Achieving Excellent Customer Service* and are coauthors of the forthcoming *Stories They Will Remember.*

The Learning Service, Ltd., 2800 Market Avenue North, Canton, OH 44714
Phone: (330) 456-2422
Fax: (330) 456-8944

E-mail: info@thelearningservice.com
Web site: www.thelearningservice.com

Kristin Anderson

(Activity 49)

Kristin Anderson is president of Say What? Consulting. With a focus on customer service management, Say What? Consulting works with individuals and organizations to ensure that what employees say/do/decide in the moment matches what the organization stands for. This is done through keynote speeches, facilitated workshops, and one-on-one coaching.

Kristin is coauthor of four books in the Best-selling Knock Your Socks Off Service series. Her newest book, *Customer Relationship Management,* was recently published by McGraw-Hill and is coauthored by Carol Kerr of Kerr Associates. Whether assisting a hospital in moving from a reputation of cold indifference to one of warmth and caring, working with a national restaurant chain on internal communication and service training, or helping a mom-and-pop retailer convey their service dedication to their staff, Say What? Consulting is committed to producing results.

President, Say What? Consulting, 2426 117th Street, Burnsville, MN 55337
Phone: (952) 920-2628
E-mail: Kristin@KristinAnderson.com
Web site: www.KristinAnderson.com

Joanne Carlson

(Activity 16, 41)

Joanne Carlson is an accomplished training consultant with more than 20 years of experience in consulting, instructional design, training program development, and project management. She is knowledgeable in the principles of adult learning and experienced in applying those principles to audiences from a wide variety of industries.

Her extensive design and consulting experience gives Joanne expertise in properly blending product knowledge and selling skills information into company-specific training applications.

Carlson Learning and Design, Inc., 13131 Galleria Place, Apple Valley, MN 55124
Phone: (952) 891-4691
Fax: (952) 953-4881
E-mail: Jocarlson@aol.com

William (Bill) E. Connor

(Activity 5, 45)

Bill E. Connor is the owner of Improved Business Performance (IBP) and a veteran of more than 30 years in the world of fast-paced production operations. With the skills learned as a teacher, production operator, supervisor, production planner, safety manager, and internal consultant for two divisions in a global manufacturing company, Bill has the innate ability to see and help others see how performance can be improved.

Whether it is simply improving an associate's communications or time management skills or something more complex such as suggesting workplace redesign, IBP has the tools to make a difference. Improved Business Performance offers free initial consultation in Ohio to determine the need and applicability of solutions. Life is full of obstacle illusions. Let us remove those that are keeping your business from reaching the pinnacle of performance.

Improved Business Performance, Tallmadge, Ohio 44278
Phone: (330) 630-3991

Jerry Drake
(Activity 32)
Jerry Drake attended Baldwin-Wallace College in Berea, Ohio, as well as the University of Maryland, where he majored in Business Administration. He has held various industrial sales positions in the industrial, chemical, and machinery fields and has 20 years' tenure with Liquid Control Corp. He is responsible for the worldwide promotion of the company's machines for lamination, coating, filtration, and medical markets.

Nancy Friedman
(Activities 2, 8, 22)
Nancy Friedman, the Telephone Doctor®, is one of America's most sought after speakers on customer service and telephone skills. She is a keynote speaker at association meetings and corporate gatherings. She is also the spokesperson in the Telephone Doctor® video-based–training programs. Nancy has authored four books (*Customer Service Nightmares, Telephone Skills from A to Z, Telemarketing Tips from A to Z,* and *How to Develop Your Own CUSTOMER SERVICE TRAINING Program*).

Telephone Doctor®, Customer Service Training, 30 Hollenberg Court, St. Louis, MO 63044
Phone: (314) 291-1012
Fax: (314) 291-3710
E-mail: nancy@telephonedoctor.com
Web site; www.telephonedoctor.com

Grant Holmes
(Activity 44)
Grant Holmes is the founder and president of Speak2You, Inc. Its focus is transforming organizational culture, one perception at a time.

Leadership & Team Building Development, 342 Leonard Avenue, NW, Massillon, Ohio 44646
Phone: (330) 327-5208
Fax: (330) 479-2991
E-mail: grant@speak2you.com
Web site: www.speak2you.com

Sue Stanek

(Activity 19)

Sue Stanek, Ph.D., has been helping organizations achieve their business goals through the development of people for more than 20 years. Sue combines her business experience with an M.A. in Adult Learning and a Ph.D. in Training and Development. Sue's experience includes serving internally within two national healthcare organizations as their training and development director, working as a product manager for Wilson Learning, providing customer training and development solutions for Fortune 500 companies through BI Performance Services, and most recently, focusing her contribution to organizations as a consultant of training and organization development solutions. Sue partners with businesses in the areas of strategic planning, leadership development, team building, sales and service development, and emotional intelligence.

8117 West 96 Street, Bloomington, MN 55438
Phone: (952) 943-2136
E-mail: suestanek@aol.com

Amy S. Tolbert

(Activities 16, 19, 41)

Amy S. Tolbert, Ph.D., develops multicultural organizations and individuals by bringing cutting-edge topics, such as fun/results-driven diversity initiatives, the leadership within, managing to style, and creating breakthrough teams, to you. She is a principal of Effecting Creative Change in Organizations (ECCO International), which specializes in creating a new sense of spirit and preparing people and organizations for sustainability in an ever-changing environment through e-learning, technology, and facilitated learning. Effecting Creative Change in Organization partners with businesses in the areas of diversity/cross-cultural education, leadership, communication, and bringing e-learning strategies to life.

Principal, ECCO International, 1519 McClung Drive, St. Paul, MN 55112
Phone: (651) 636-0838
E-mail: Amy Tolbert@ECCOInternational.com
Web site: www.ECCOInternational.com

INDEX